Inquiries in
Rational Emotive Behaviour
Therapy

Inquiries in Rational Emotive Behaviour Therapy

Windy Dryden

SAGE Publications
London • Thousand Oaks • New Delhi

First published 1996

 SAGE Publications Ltd
6 Bonhill Street
London EC2A 4PU

SAGE Publications Inc
2455 Teller Road
Thousand Oaks, California 91320

SAGE Publications India Pvt Ltd
32, M-Block Market
Greater Kailash – I
New Delhi 110 048

British Library Cataloguing in Publication data

A catalogue record for this book is available from the British Library

ISBN 0 7619 5130 X
ISBN 0 7619 5131 8 (pbk)

Library of Congress catalog card number 96–068419

Typeset by Mayhew Typesetting, Rhayader, Powys
Printed in Great Britain by The Cromwell Press Ltd,
Broughton Gifford, Melksham, Wiltshire

Contents

To Joyce Rothschild

Preface

In 1993, Albert Ellis decided to change the name of Rational-Emotive Therapy (RET) to Rational Emotive Behaviour Therapy (REBT). Other changes in REBT have also been occurring. REBT theory is being refined and its practice is being expanded. This volume is devoted to the changes in REBT that I have helped to initiate, develop or simplify.

The book opens with a brief overview of basic REBT theory and practice so that readers new to REBT can get their bearings and understand the material presented in the rest of the book. Chapter 2 compares RET *circa* 1962, when Ellis published his seminal and oft-quoted book, *Reason and Emotion in Psychotherapy*, with REBT about thirty years on just before the publication in 1994 of the revised and expanded version of *Reason and Emotion*. Chapters 3–6 are devoted to theoretical developments, while Chapters 7–9 concentrate on practical innovations. The closing chapters focus on innovations in REBT supervision that were either developed earlier and are only now making their mark (Chapters 10 and 11) or have arisen from more recent developments in practice (Chapter 12).

REBT is now really 'taking off' in Britain and Europe. I am running Europe's first Master's course in REBT at Goldsmiths College, University of London, the Association for Rational Emotive Behaviour Therapists has come into being in Britain, is flourishing and publishes a vibrant new REBT journal. The European REBT training centres are training increasing numbers of therapists. A wind of change is gathering force in the world of REBT. This book is a personal example of this change.

Acknowledgements

The author and publishers wish to thank the following for permission to use copyright material:

The Association for Rational-Emotive Therapists for articles by Windy Dryden from *The Rational Emotive Behaviour Therapist*: 'When Musts Are Not Enough', 1994, 2(2); 'Who is Suitable for Brief REBT?', 1995, 3(1); 'Paradoxical REBT: A Humorous Intervention', 1994, 2(2); and by Robin Yapp and Windy Dryden for 'The Role of Concurrent Beliefs in Emotional Disturbance', 1995 3(1), and 'Supervision of REBT Therapists', 1994, 2(1); Plenum Publishing Corporation for Windy Dryden, 'Reason and Emotion in Psychotherapy: Thirty Years On', *Journal of Rational-Emotive & Cognitive Behavior Therapy*, 1994, 12(2); Routledge for Windy Dryden, 'Teaching the Principles of Unconditional Self-Acceptance in a Structured, Group Setting' from *New Directions in Counselling*, ed. R. Bayne, I. Horton and J. Bimrose, 1996; Whurr Publishers Ltd for Chapters 6 and 8 from Windy Dryden, *Invitation to Rational-Emotive Psychology*, (1994); and Windy Dryden, 'Using REBT in the Supervision of Counsellors' from *Dryden on Counselling, Vol. 3: Training and Supervision*, 1991; John Wiley & Sons for Chapter 2 from Windy Dryden, *Brief Rational Emotive Behaviour Therapy*, 1995. Every effort has been made to trace all the copyright holders but if any have been inadvertently overlooked the publishers will be pleased to make the necessary arrangement at the first opportunity.

1

The Basic Principles and Practice of Rational Emotive Behaviour Therapy (REBT): A Brief Overview

In this chapter I will outline the basic principles and practice of REBT. In particular, I will tailor my discussion to the concepts that you, the reader, will need to understand in order to get the most out of this book. This chapter will therefore be selective rather than comprehensive. For an up-to-date and full presentation of the theory and practice of REBT, you are advised to consult Ellis (1994). The topics I will cover in this chapter concern: (1) the two principles of emotional responsibility; (2) the two types of psychological disturbance; (3) the REBT model of healthy and unhealthy negative emotions; (4) the principle of psychological interactionism; and (5) the process of therapeutic change. I will also introduce the now famous ABCDEs of REBT.

The Two Principles of Emotional Responsibility

If I have learned anything about clients from my twenty years' experience as a counsellor and therapist, it is that at the beginning of therapy clients adhere to what might be called the principle of emotional irresponsibility. In a nutshell, they tend to believe that the way they feel is caused by factors outside of themselves. This is by no means a characteristic of clients alone. If you listen to how people talk about emotional issues, you will hear that talk peppered with phrases such as: 'He made me so angry', 'It really made me anxious', 'If they do that, they will make me very depressed', etc.

As these statements show, we tend to believe that our emotions such as anger, anxiety and depression are caused directly by the actions of others and by life events or what I call the 'its' of this world. This 'naive' view of the determinants of human emotion can be contrasted with the cognitive view of human emotion.

This chapter is a modified version of one originally published in W. Dryden, *Brief Rational Emotive Behaviour Therapy*. Chichester: Wiley, 1995.

THE GENERAL PRINCIPLE OF EMOTIONAL RESPONSIBILITY

As any introductory book on psychology will tell you, there has been a cognitive revolution in mainstream psychology, which used to be dominated by behavioural principles. This cognitive revolution stresses the importance of the way we transform the information that we detect with our senses. It claims that such transformations have a critical influence on the way we feel and act. This idea has permeated all areas of psychology, including psychotherapy and counselling. Actually, this is far from a novel idea, since the Stoic philosopher Epictetus said many years ago that we are disturbed not by things themselves, but by the views we take of them. This statement nicely describes what I have called the *general* principle of emotional responsibility (Dryden, 1995) which can be stated more formally thus: *We are largely, but not exclusively, responsible for the way we feel and act by the views we take of the events in our lives.* To say that we are exclusively responsible for the way we feel and act is a dogmatic position which negates the influence of these events and, as we shall see presently, REBT takes a stand against dogmatic positions. The REBT general principle of emotional responsibility states that events contribute to the way we feel and act, but do not cause these reactions which, as I have said, are largely determined by our views of events.

THE SPECIFIC PRINCIPLE OF EMOTIONAL RESPONSIBILITY

At the heart of the general principle of emotional responsibility is the concept of 'view'. While this points to the importance of understanding the cognitions or thoughts that your clients have about themselves, other people and the world, it is in itself too vague to provide you with the detailed information that you need as a therapist to understand precisely how clients disturb themselves and what you need to focus on to help them overcome their emotional problems. For such detailed information you need to understand the second principle of emotional responsibility – what I have called the *specific* principle of emotional responsibility (Dryden, 1995).

The specific principle of emotional responsibility is so termed because it specifies precisely the kinds of 'views' that are at the core of psychological disturbance and, as importantly, the kinds of 'views' that are at the core of psychological well-being. In outlining the REBT position on this issue, I will present below four belief pairs. The first belief in the pair will be that associated with psychological health and the second that associated with psychological disturbance. In the language of Rational Emotive Behaviour Therapy, the first are known as rational beliefs and the second, irrational beliefs. Before I present the four belief pairs that describe precisely how we disturb ourselves about self, others and life conditions and what we would have to think in order to be healthy instead, let me briefly discuss the terms 'rational' and 'irrational' as they are used in REBT theory.

THE MEANING OF THE TERMS 'RATIONAL' AND 'IRRATIONAL' IN REBT

The term 'rational' in REBT theory refers to beliefs which are (1) flexible; (2) consistent with reality; (3) logical; and which (4) promote the person's psychological well-being and aid her pursuit of her personally meaningful goals. In contrast, the term 'irrational' in REBT theory refers to beliefs which are (1) rigid; (2) inconsistent with reality; (3) illogical; and which (4) interfere with the person's psychological well-being and get in the way of her pursuing her personally meaningful goals. Having outlined the meaning of the terms 'rational' and 'irrational' as they refer to beliefs, I will distinguish among four types of cognition before discussing the four belief pairs which embody the specific principle of emotional responsibility and which delineate precisely the 'views' that people hold about self, others and the world that lead either to psychological well-being or to psychological disturbance.

THE FOUR TYPES OF COGNITION

REBT therapists distinguish among four types of cognition: descriptions, interpretations, inferences and evaluations (Wessler and Wessler, 1980; Dryden, 1994). I will briefly discuss these different types of cognitions since an understanding of the differences among them will help you to understand fully the specific REBT principle of emotional responsibility.

The first type of cognition, *description*, seeks to describe the nature of a stimulus without adding any non-observable meaning. As such, descriptions can be accurate (e.g. 'The man is walking along the street' when this is so) or inaccurate (e.g. 'The man is running along the street' when, in fact, he was walking).

The second type of cognition, *interpretation*, goes beyond the data at hand, but is non-evaluative. Thus, we make interpretations in non-emotional episodes, i.e. when our emotions are not involved (e.g. 'The man is going to the postbox to post a letter.' This statement is an interpretation because it goes beyond the data at hand – I do not know whether or not the person is going to post a letter; and because my emotions are not involved).

The third type of cognition, *inference*, also goes beyond the data at hand and is partly evaluative. Thus, we make inferences in emotional episodes, i.e. when out emotions are involved. Even though our inferences influence the type of emotion we experience (e.g. sadness or depression as opposed to remorse or guilt), they do not fully account for our precise emotion (i.e. they do not explain why we feel depression as opposed to sadness, or guilt as opposed to remorse). That is why I say that inferences are partly evaluative. An example of an inference might be 'The man is going to the post office to post a letter to my boss that may lead me to lose my job.' This statement is an inference because it goes beyond the data at hand – I do not know whether or not the person is going to post a letter to my boss that may lead me to lose my job; and because my emotions are involved. Thus, I may feel anxious or concern.

It is important to note that interpretations and inferences are similar in that both are hunches about reality rather than factual. As such, they need to be tested against the available evidence.

The fourth type of cognition, *evaluation*, as its name implies is fully evaluative and is centrally involved in our emotional experiences. Most often, an evaluation involves a person making a positive or a negative appraisal. In addition an appraisal can be neutral, as in the statement: 'I don't care whether or not I pass my driving test.' The following four belief pairs can be viewed as evaluative beliefs since they are evaluative in nature and they point to what people believe.

THE FOUR BELIEF PAIRS

Preferences vs. Musts

Evaluative beliefs which are flexible in nature are often couched in the form of preferences (or their synonyms, e.g. wishes, wants, desires). Preferences can point to what we want to happen (e.g. 'I want to pass my driving test') or to what we do not want to occur (e.g. 'I don't want to get into trouble with my boss'). However, to understand the full meaning of a preference, its non-dogmatic nature needs to be made explicit in the person's statement. To take the two examples I have just mentioned, we can tell that they are really preferences thus:

• 'I want to pass my driving test, *but* I don't have to do so.'

• 'I don't want to get into trouble with my boss, *but* there's no reason why I must not do so.'

The reason why it is so important for preferences to be put in their full form is that if they are expressed in their partial form (e.g. 'I want to pass my driving test'), then it is easy for us to change it *implicitly* to a dogmatic must [e.g. 'I want to pass my driving test (and therefore I have to do so)']. As I have shown elsewhere, the stronger our preferences, the more likely we are, if left to our own devices, to change these preferences into musts (Dryden, 1994).

Preferences are rational because they are (1) flexible (i.e. they allow for what is not preferred to occur); (2) consistent with reality (i.e. they are consistent with the inner reality of the person's preferences); (3) logical; and they (4) promote the person's psychological well-being and aid her pursuit of her personally meaningful goals (i.e. they lead to healthy negative emotions when the person's preferences aren't met, which in turn facilitate effective problem-solving or constructive adjustment if changes cannot be made).

Evaluative beliefs which are rigid in nature are often couched in the form of musts (or their synonyms, e.g. absolute shoulds, have-tos, got-tos, etc.). Musts indicate that we believe that what we want absolutely has to occur (e.g. 'I absolutely have to pass my driving test') or that what we don't want absolutely should not happen (e.g. 'I must not get into trouble with my boss').

Musts are irrational because they are (1) inflexible (i.e. they do not allow for what must happen not to occur); (2) inconsistent with reality (if there was a law of the universe that says I must pass my driving test, I could not possibly fail. This law, of course, does not exist); (3) illogical (i.e. they do not logically follow from the person's preferences); and they (4) interfere with the person's psychological well-being and get in the way of her pursuing her personally meaningful goals (i.e. they lead to unhealthy negative emotions when the person's demands aren't met, which in turn impede effective problem-solving or constructive adjustment if changes cannot be made).

Albert Ellis (1994), the founder of REBT, holds that non-dogmatic preferences are at the very core of psychological health and that three other major rational beliefs are derived from these preferences. Similarly, Ellis believes that dogmatic musts are at the very core of emotional disturbance and that three other irrational beliefs are derived from these musts. While other REBT theorists hold different views on this issue, I will take Ellis's position in this book. As such, the following three belief pairs should be regarded as derivatives from preferences and musts respectively.

Anti-awfulizing vs. Awfulizing

Anti-awfulizing evaluative beliefs are rational in the sense that they are first and foremost non-dogmatic. These beliefs, which in their full form are expressed thus: 'It would be very bad if I failed my driving test, but it wouldn't be awful', are flexibly located on a continuum ranging from 0–99.9 per cent badness. The stronger a person's unmet preference, the higher her evaluation will be placed on this continuum. However, an anti-awfulizing belief cannot reach 100 per cent, since as Smokey Robinson's mother used to tell her young son: 'From the time you are born 'til you ride in the hearse, there's nothing so bad that it couldn't be worse.' In this sense, an anti-awfulizing belief is consistent with reality. This belief is also logical since it makes sense in the context of the person's preference. Finally, it is constructive since it will help the person take effective action if the negative event that the person is facing can be changed and it will aid the person to make a healthy adjustment if the situation cannot be changed.

Awfulizing beliefs, on the other hand, are irrational in the sense that they are first and foremost dogmatic. They are rigidly located on a magical 'horror' continuum ranging from 101 per cent badness to infinity. They are couched in such terms as 'It's horrible that . . .', 'It's terrible that . . .', 'It's awful that . . .' and 'It's the end of the world that . . .'. When a person is awfulizing, he literally believes at that moment that nothing could be worse. In this sense, an awfulizing belief is inconsistent with reality. This belief is also illogical since it is a nonsensical conclusion from the person's implicit rational belief (e.g., 'Because it would be very bad if I failed my driving test it would therefore be awful if this happened'). Finally, an awfulizing belief is constructive since it will interfere with the person taking effective action if the negative event that the person is facing can be changed and it will stop the person from making a healthy adjustment if the situation cannot be changed.

High Frustration Tolerance (HFT) vs. Low Frustration Tolerance (LFT)

High frustration tolerance beliefs are rational in the sense that they are again primarily flexible and not grossly exaggerated. These beliefs are expressed in their full form, thus: 'Failing my driving test would be difficult to tolerate, but I could stand it.' The stronger a person's unmet preference, the more difficult it would be for her to tolerate this situation, but if she holds an HFT belief it would still be tolerable. In this sense, an HFT belief is consistent with reality. It is also logical since it again makes sense in the context of the person's preference. Finally, like a preference and an anti-awfulizing belief, it is constructive since it will help the person take effective action if the negative event that the person is facing can be changed and it will encourage the person to make a healthy adjustment if the situation cannot be changed.

Low frustration tolerance beliefs, on the other hand, are irrational in the sense that they are first and foremost grossly exaggerated. They are couched in such terms as 'I can't stand it . . .', 'I can't bear it . . .', 'It's intolerable . . .'. When a person has a low frustration tolerance belief, she means one of two things: she will disintegrate, or she will never experience any happiness again. Since these two statements are obviously untrue, an LFT belief is inconsistent with reality. It is also illogical since it is a nonsensical conclusion from the person's implicit rational belief (e.g. 'Because it would be very bad if I failed my driving test, I couldn't stand it if I did fail'). Finally, like musts and awfulizing beliefs, it is unconstructive since it will interfere with the person taking effective action if the negative event that the person is facing can be changed and it will stop the person from making a healthy adjustment if the situation cannot be changed.

Self/Other-Acceptance vs. Self/Other-Downing

Acceptance beliefs are rational in the sense that they are again primarily flexible. In discussing acceptance beliefs, I will focus on self-acceptance, although exactly the same arguments apply to other-acceptance. When a person accepts herself, she acknowledges that she is a unique, ongoing, ever-changing fallible human being with good, bad and neutral aspects. In short, she is far too complex to merit a single, global rating. Self-esteem, on the other hand, is based on the idea that it is possible to assign a single rating to the 'self'. An example of a self-acceptance belief expressed in its full form follows: 'If I fail my driving test due to my own errors, I could still accept myself as a fallible human being who has failed on this occasion. I would not be a failure.' As this example shows, a self-acceptance belief is consistent with the reality of a person being too complex to merit a single global rating. A self-acceptance belief is also logical since it is logical for a person to conclude that he is fallible if he makes errors. Finally, as with the other three rational beliefs I have discussed, a self-acceptance belief is constructive since it will once again help the person take effective action if the negative event that the person is facing can be changed and it will also aid the person to make a healthy adjustment if the situation cannot be changed.

Self-downing beliefs, on the other hand, are irrational in the sense that they take a rigid, grossly exaggerated, view of the 'self'. They are couched in such terms as 'I am bad', 'I am a failure', 'I am less worthy', 'I am undeserving'. When a person holds a self-downing belief, he is working on the assumption that it is legitimate to assign a global (in this case negative) rating to his 'self'. Since this, in fact, cannot legitimately be done, a self-downing belief is inconsistent with reality. It is also illogical since in making a self-downing statement, the person is making the 'part–whole error', i.e. he is correctly rating an aspect of himself, but then he rates his entire self based on the evaluation of the part. Finally, like the other three irrational beliefs I have discussed, a self-downing belief is unconstructive since it will interfere with the person taking effective action if the negative event that the person is facing can be changed and it will stop the person from making a healthy adjustment if the situation cannot be changed.

Having now introduced the four rational beliefs and four irrational beliefs deemed by REBT theory to lie at the core of psychological well-being and psychological disturbance respectively, let me formally state the specific principle of emotional responsibility:

The REBT specific principle of emotional responsibility states that events contribute to the way we feel and act, but do not cause these reactions, which are largely determined by our rational or irrational beliefs about these events.

The Two Types of Psychological Disturbance

There are two different types of such disturbance: ego disturbance and discomfort disturbance.

EGO DISTURBANCE

As the name implies, ego disturbance concerns psychological problems that ultimately relate to the person's view of herself. Sometimes such problems are obviously related to the self, as when a person is depressed and says, almost without prompting, 'Because I failed my driving test, I am a failure.' At other times, ego disturbance is not so transparent. For example, a person might claim to be anxious about travelling by underground. Put like that, it is not at all obvious that the person's problems may be an example of ego disturbance. However, on much closer examination, this turns out to be the case when the person reveals that he is anxious about travelling by tube because he might get panicky and, as stated in his own words, 'make a fool of myself by passing out'. As will be discussed later, effective therapy is based on an accurate assessment of a client's problems, and this assessment will reveal whether or not a particular problem is related to ego disturbance.

Ego disturbance occurs when a person makes a global, negative rating of his or herself. Such ratings can be made in different areas and are related to different disorders. Let me provide a few examples to illustrate my point:

- When a person believes that she is a failure or a loser then it is likely that she will be depressed when she has failed or anxious when there exists a threat of failure which hasn't yet occurred.
- When a person believes that she is bad then it is likely that she will experience guilt.
- When a person believes that she is defective or weak then it is likely that she will experience shame.

The self-ratings that are involved in ego disturbance are usually expressed quite starkly, as in the statements: 'I am bad' or 'I am a bad person'. However, they can also be expressed more subtly as in the statements: 'I am less worthy' or 'I am undeserving'. Generally speaking, the more starkly they are expressed in the person's belief structure, the greater that person's ego disturbance will be.

Finally, as noted above (see p. 5), ego disturbance is derived from dogmatic, 'musturbatory' beliefs, as in the following example: 'I am a failure because I did not pass my driving test as I absolutely should have done'. According to this view, if the person in this example had a preferential belief about failing such as: 'I would have preferred not to have failed my driving test, but there's no reason why I absolutely should not have done', then she would be far less likely to condemn herself than she would if she held a demanding belief about failure, as shown at the beginning of this paragraph.

DISCOMFORT DISTURBANCE

As the name implies, discomfort disturbance concerns psychological problems that ultimately relate to the person's sense of comfort and discomfort. In REBT, the concepts of comfort and discomfort cover a wide range of issues. For example, they may relate to justice/injustice, fulfilment/frustration, positive feelings/negative feelings, etc. What they have in common, however, is that they do not refer to the person's view of himself. Rather, discomfort disturbance relates to the person's perceived inability to tolerate discomfort, whether this is in the area of feelings (e.g. anxiety) or life situations (e.g. unfairness).

Like ego disturbance, discomfort disturbance can be obvious or more subtle. An example of discomfort disturbance that is obvious is when a person says (and truly believes) that she can't stand waiting for the traffic lights to change. A more subtle example of discomfort disturbance is when a person says that she is afraid of failing her driving test. It might appear, at first sight, that the person's anxiety is an example of ego disturbance. However, on much closer examination, this turns out not to be the case when the person reveals that she is anxious about not getting the £1,000 that her father promised her if she passed the test. As she said, 'I couldn't bear to lose out on all the goodies I had planned to buy with the money.' This is clearly an example of discomfort disturbance. Once again, careful assessment is needed to tease out discomfort-disturbance-related irrational beliefs.

Discomfort disturbance occurs when a person's LFT beliefs come to the fore (see p. 5). Such beliefs can be held in different areas and related to different disorders. Let me provide a few examples to illustrate my point:

- When a person believes that she cannot stand being blocked or frustrated then it is likely that she will be angry.
- When a person believes that she cannot tolerate losing a prized possession then it is likely that she will experience depression if she loses it.
- When a person believes that she can't bear feeling anxious then it is likely that she will experience increased anxiety.

The evaluations involved in discomfort disturbance can be explicit, as when the person says that she cannot bear the discomfort of speaking in public. However, they can also be implicit as when people avoid facing uncomfortable situations. It is as if the person is implicitly saying 'I'll avoid that situation because I couldn't stand the discomfort of facing it.' The more widespread the person's avoidance, the greater that person's discomfort disturbance is likely to be.

Finally, as noted above, discomfort disturbance is derived from dogmatic musturbatory beliefs, as in the following example: 'I can't stand being deprived because I absolutely must get what I want.' As discussed in the section on ego disturbance, if the person in this example had a preferential belief about being deprived such as: 'I would like to get what I want, but I don't have to get it', then she would be far less likely to disturb herself about the deprivation than she would if she held a demanding belief about her failure to get what she wants.

EGO DISTURBANCE AND DISCOMFORT DISTURBANCE CAN
INTERACT

Ellis (1994) has noted that ego disturbance and discomfort disturbance can interact, often in complex ways. For example, let's suppose
that a person believes that she must do well at a job interview and if
she doesn't that means that she is less worthy than she would be
if she did well. This ego disturbance belief leads the person to feel
anxiety as the date of the interview draws near. At this point the
person becomes aware that she is feeling anxious and tells herself
implicitly that she must get rid of her anxiety straight away and that
she can't stand feeling anxious. As the result of this discomfort
disturbance belief, her anxiety increases. Realizing that she is getting
very anxious for what to her is no good reason and that she
absolutely shouldn't do this, she concludes that she is a weak,
pathetic person for getting matters out of proportion. This second
ego disturbance adds to her emotional distress, which activates a
further discomfort-related irrational belief about losing control.

It is important to note that this interaction between ego disturbance
and discomfort disturbance can occur very quickly and outside the
person's awareness. Dealing therapeutically with complex interactions between the two types of disturbance is quite difficult and
involves the therapist dealing with one link of the chain at a time.

The REBT View of Healthy and Unhealthy Negative Emotions

One of the unique contributions of REBT theory to therapeutic
practice is the distinction it makes between healthy and unhealthy
negative emotions. I have outlined this viewpoint in Table 1.1 and
suggest that you familiarize yourself thoroughly with the information it contains before you attempt to practise brief REBT. The
following is a short guide to the form and its different components. I
will start from the left-hand column (column 1) and move to the
right-hand column (column 6).

COLUMN 1: EMOTION

In this column, I provide pairs of emotions, and in doing so I use
the REBT emotional lexicon. As you will see from the next column,
the first emotion of the pair is unhealthy, while the second is the

alternative healthy negative emotion. I should stress that while it is not essential to use the emotional lexicon in the precise way that it is used in REBT, it is important to develop a shared language with each of your clients so that you both have an agreed way of differentiating between healthy and unhealthy negative emotions.

COLUMN 2: HEALTHY OR UNHEALTHY

In this column, I indicate which of the two negative emotions is unhealthy and which is healthy. As noted above, the first of the pair is unhealthy and the second, healthy.

By a negative emotion I mean an emotion which is unpleasant to experience. I want to stress that I am not making a moral judgement when I refer to an emotion as negative. Having emphasized this, let me differentiate between a healthy negative emotion and its unhealthy counterpart.

A healthy negative emotion is an emotion which can be seen as an adaptive response to an actual or inferred negative event in that it helps the person to change what can be changed and to adjust constructively to what can't be changed. It encourages the person to pursue her personally meaningful goals by encouraging her to think (see column 5) and act (see column 6) in helpful ways.

In contrast, an unhealthy negative emotion is an emotion which can be seen as a maladaptive response to an actual or inferred negative event in that it gets in the way of the person changing what can be changed and impedes her from adjusting constructively to what can't be changed. It interferes with the person's attempts to pursue her personally meaningful goals and does so by influencing her to think (see column 5) and act (see column 6) in unhelpful ways.

COLUMN 3: INFERENCE IN RELATION TO ONE'S PERSONAL DOMAIN

Earlier in this chapter (see p. 4) I defined an inference as a cognition which goes beyond the data at hand and occurs in an emotional episode. It differs from an interpretation in one important respect. An inference is present when a person experiences an emotion, while an interpretation occurs in a non-emotional episode. Moreover, an inference gives meaning to the observable data, but in a way that may be accurate or inaccurate. Given its involvement in a person's emotional episode, an inference is partly evaluative in that it plays an important part in determining which emotional pair a person experiences (see column 1), but it is not fully evaluative in that it cannot determine which of the two emotions within the pair a person will experience.

In order to understand inferences fully, it is important to grasp the meaning of the term 'personal domain' since inferences are formed in relation to an individual's personal domain. Beck (1976) has said that a personal domain contains those tangible and intangible objects in which the person has an involvement. As shown in the previous section, REBT theory distinguishes between ego and comfort aspects of the personal domain although, as I have stressed, these two aspects frequently interact.

Column 3 therefore lists the most prominent inferences that are made by people when they experience anxiety or concern, depression or sadness, unhealthy anger or healthy anger, and so on. It should be clear from this column that since the same inference is involved, for example in anxiety and concern, changing this inference will mean that the person will experience neither unhealthy anxiety nor healthy concern. The first effect is certainly acceptable, but the second isn't, since it is often important that the person reacts to threat with concern even if it can be shown on a given occasion that no threat exists. Given this, we need to find a more profound and longer-lasting way of helping a person to overcome his unhealthy anxiety while encouraging him to experience healthy concern. It is for this reason that REBT therapists encourage their clients to accept temporarily that their distorted inferences are true. Doing so helps both therapist and client to identify the irrational beliefs which, according to REBT theory, are the most important determinants of clients' unhealthy negative emotions.

COLUMN 4: TYPE OF BELIEF

In the first section of this chapter I distinguished between rational beliefs and irrational beliefs. If you recall, rational beliefs are flexible, consistent with reality, logical and help the person to pursue his personally meaningful goals. They take the form of preferences, anti-awfulizing evaluations, high frustration tolerance and self/other acceptance. Irrational beliefs, on the other hand, are dogmatic, inconsistent with reality, illogical and interfere with the person's achievement of personally meaningful goals. They take the form of musts, awfulizing evaluations, low frustration tolerance and self/other downing.

According to REBT theory and as shown in Table 1.1, irrational beliefs are at the core of unhealthy negative emotions, while rational beliefs are at the core of healthy negative emotions. Thus, the type of belief has a crucial effect on which of the two emotions within a pair a person will experience. Given the central role that irrational beliefs play in determining emotional disturbance, it is

Table 1.1 *A diagrammatic summary of healthy and unhealthy negative emotions*

Emotion	Healthy or unhealthy	Inference[1] in relation to personal domain[2]	Type of belief	Cognitive consequences	Action tendencies
Anxiety (ego or discomfort)	Unhealthy	• Threat or danger	Irrational	• Overestimates negative features of the threat • Underestimates ability to cope with the threat • Creates an even more negative threat in one's mind • Has more task-irrelevant thoughts than in concern	• To withdraw physically from the threat • To withdraw mentally from the threat • To ward off the threat (e.g. by superstitious behaviour) • To tranquillize feelings • To seek reassurance
Concern	Healthy	• Threat or danger	Rational	• Views the threat realistically • Realistic appraisal of ability to cope with the threat • Does not create an even more negative threat in one's mind • Has more task-relevant thoughts than in anxiety	• To face up to the threat • To deal with the threat constructively
Depression (ego or discomfort)	Unhealthy	• Loss (with implications for future) • Failure	Irrational	• Only sees negative aspects of the loss or failure • Thinks of other losses and failures that one has experienced • Thinks one is unable to help self (helplessness) • Only sees pain and blackness in the future (hopelessness)	• To withdraw from reinforcements • To withdraw into oneself • To create an environment consistent with feelings • To attempt to terminate feelings of depression in self-destructive ways

Sadness	Healthy	• Loss (with implications for future) • Failure	Rational	• Able to see both negative and positive aspects of the loss or failure • Less likely to think of other losses and failures than when depressed • Able to help self • Able to look into the future with hope	• To express feelings about the loss or failure and talk about these to significant ones • To seek out reinforcements after a period of mourning
Unhealthy Anger	Unhealthy	• Frustration • Self or other transgresses personal rule • Threat to self-esteem	Irrational	• Overestimates the extent to which the other person acted deliberately • Sees malicious intent in the motives of others • Self seen as definitely right; other(s) seen as definitely wrong • Unable to see the other person's point of view • Plots to exact revenge	• To attack the other physically • To attack the other verbally • To attack the other passive-aggressively • To displace the attack on to another person, animal or object • To withdraw aggressively • To recruit allies against the other
Healthy Anger	Healthy	• Frustration • Self or other transgresses personal rule • Threat to self-esteem	Rational	• Does not overestimate the extent to which the other person acted deliberately • Does not see malicious intent in the motives of the other • Does not see self as definitely right and the other as definitely wrong • Able to see the other's point of view • Does not plot to exact revenge	• To assert self with the other • To request, but not demand, behavioural change from the other

continued overleaf

Table 1.1 (continued)

Emotion	Healthy or unhealthy	Inference[1] in relation to personal domain[2]	Type of belief	Cognitive consequences	Action tendencies
Guilt	Unhealthy	• Violation of moral code (sin of commission) • Failure to live up to moral code (sin of omission) • Hurts the feelings of a significant other	Irrational	• Assumes that one has definitely committed the sin • Assumes more personal responsibility than the situation warrants • Assigns far less responsibility to others than is warranted • Does not think of mitigating factors • Thinks that one will receive retribution	• To escape from the unhealthy pain of guilt in self-defeating ways • To beg for forgiveness from the person wronged • To promise unrealistically that she will not 'sin' again • To punish self physically or by deprivation • To disclaim responsibility for wrongdoing
Remorse	Healthy	• Violation of moral code (sin of commission) • Failure to live up to moral code (sin of omission) • Hurts the feelings of a significant other	Rational	• Considers behaviour in context and with understanding in making a final judgement concerning whether one has 'sinned' • Assumes appropriate level of personal responsibility • Assigns appropriate level of responsibility to others • Takes into account mitigating factors • Does not think one will receive retribution	• To face up to the healthy pain that accompanies the realization that one has sinned • To ask, but not beg for forgiveness • To understand reasons for wrongdoing and act on one's understanding • To atone for the sin by taking a penalty • To make appropriate amends • No tendency to make excuses for one's behaviour or enact other defensive behaviour

Emotion		Belief		Cognitions	Action Tendencies
Shame	Unhealthy	• Something shameful has been revealed about self (or group with whom one identifies) by self or others • Others will look down or shun self (or group with whom one identifies)	Irrational	• Overestimates the 'shamefulness' of the information revealed • Overestimates the likelihood that the judging group will notice or be interested in the information • Overestimates the degree of disapproval self (or reference group) will receive • Overestimates the length of time any disapproval will last	• To remove self from the 'gaze' of others • To isolate self from others • To save face by attacking other(s) who have 'shamed' self • To defend threatened self-esteem in self-defeating ways • To ignore attempts by others to restore social equilibrium
Regret	Healthy	• Something shameful has been revealed about self (or group with whom one identifies) by self or others • Others will look down or shun self (or group with whom one identifies)	Rational	• Sees information revealed in a compassionate self-accepting context • Is realistic about the likelihood that the judging group will notice or be interested in the information • Is realistic about the degree of disapproval self (or reference group) will receive • Is realistic about the length of time any disapproval will last	• To continue to participate actively in social interaction • To respond to attempts of others to restore social equilibrium

continued overleaf

Table 1.1 (continued)

Emotion	Healthy or unhealthy	Inference[1] in relation to personal domain[2]	Type of belief	Cognitive consequences	Action tendencies
Hurt	Unhealthy	• Other treats self badly (self undeserving)	Irrational	• Overestimates the unfairness of the other person's behaviour • Other perceived as showing lack of care or indifference • Self seen as alone, uncared for or misunderstood • Tends to think of past 'hurts' • Thinks that the other has to put things right of own accord first	• To shut down communication channel with the other • To criticize the other without disclosing what one feels hurt about
Disappoint-ment	Healthy	• Other treats self badly (self undeserving)	Rational	• Is realistic about the degree of unfairness of the other person's behaviour • Other perceived as acting badly rather than as uncaring or indifferent • Self not seen as alone, uncared for and misunderstood • Less likely to think of past hurts than when hurt • Doesn't think that the other has to make the first move	• To communicate one's feelings to the other directly • To influence the other person to act in a fairer manner

Emotion		Inference theme		Thinking	Action tendencies
Jealousy	Unhealthy	Threat to relationship with partner from another person	Irrational	• Tends to see threats to one's relationship when none really exists • Thinks the loss of one's relationship is imminent • Misconstrues one's partner's ordinary conversations as having romantic or sexual connotations • Constructs visual images of partner's infidelity • If partner admits to finding another attractive, believes that the other is seen as more attractive than self and that one's partner will leave self for this other person	• To seek constant reassurance that one is loved • To monitor the actions and feelings of one's partner • To search for evidence that one's partner is involved with someone else • To attempt to restrict the movements or activities of one's partner • To set tests which partner has to pass • To retaliate for partner's presumed infidelity • To sulk
Concern for one's relationship	Healthy	Threat to relationship with partner from another person	Rational	• Tends not to see threats to one's relationship when none exists • Does not think that the loss of one's relationship is imminent • Does not misconstrue ordinary conversations between partner and other men/women • Does not construct visual images of partner's infidelity • Accepts that partner will find others attractive but does not see this as a threat	• To allow partner to express love without seeking reassurance • To allow partner freedom without monitoring his/her feelings, actions and whereabouts • To allow him/her to show natural interest in members of the opposite sex without setting tests

continued overleaf

Table 1.1 (continued)

Emotion	Healthy or unhealthy	Inference[1] in relation to personal domain[2]	Type of belief	Cognitive consequences	Action tendencies
Unhealthy envy	Unhealthy	• Another person possesses and enjoys something desirable that the person does not have	Irrational	• Tends to denigrate the value of the desired possession • Tries to convince self that one is happy with one's possessions (although one is not) • Thinks about how to acquire the desired possession regardless of its usefulness • Thinks about how to deprive the other person of the desired possession	• To disparage verbally the person who has the desired possession • To disparage verbally the desired possession • To take away the desired possession from the other (either so that one will have it or the other is deprived of it) • To spoil or destroy the desired possession so that the other person does not have it
Healthy envy	Healthy	• Another person possesses and enjoys something desirable that the person does not have	Rational	• Honestly admits to oneself how one desires the desired possession • Does not try to convince self that one is happy with one's possessions when one is not • Thinks about how to obtain the desired possession because one desires it for healthy reasons • Can allow the person to have and enjoy the desired possession without denigrating the person of the possession	• To obtain the desired possession if it is truly what one wants

---

[1] Inference: personally significant hunch that goes beyond observable reality and which gives meaning to it; may be accurate or inaccurate.

[2] Personal domain: The objects – tangible and intangible – in which a person has an involvement (Beck, 1976). REBT theory distinguishes between ego and comfort aspects of the personal domain although those aspects frequently interact.

beliefs (rather than inferences), and more precisely irrational beliefs, that are the initial target of change in REBT. Once you have helped your client to change his irrational beliefs to rational beliefs, then you can help him to challenge other kinds of faulty cognitions, such as distorted inferences.

Figure 1.2 shows how healthy negative emotions stem from the interaction of inferences and rational beliefs and how healthy negative emotions stem from the interaction of these same inferences and rational beliefs.

Inference × rational beliefs = healthy negative emotion

Inference × irrational beliefs = unhealthy negative emotion

Figure 1.2 *Healthy negative emotions stem from an interaction between an inference and rational beliefs. Unhealthy negative emotions stem from an interaction between the same inference and irrational beliefs.*

COLUMN 5: COGNITIVE CONSEQUENCES

Once a person experiences an unhealthy negative emotion because she is holding an irrational belief about a negative activating event, then she will have a tendency to think in certain overly negative, unhelpful ways. On the other hand, when that person has a healthy negative emotion because she is holding a rational belief about that same negative event, then she will tend to think in more constructive ways. It is important to understand these cognitive consequences of rational or irrational beliefs because they have an effect on the person's subsequent approach to problem-solving.

COLUMN 6: ACTION TENDENCIES

In addition to affecting a person's thinking processes, beliefs also have a decided influence on the ways in which that person will tend to act. When a person is thinking irrationally and experiencing unhealthy negative emotions, she will tend to act in self-defeating and goal-impeding ways. However, when she is thinking rationally and is experiencing healthy negative emotions, then she will tend to act in more self-enhancing and goal-directed ways.

Just because a person has a tendency to act in a certain way does not mean that he will always act in accordance with this action tendency. It is almost always possible for a person to go against his action tendency and doing so is very important if he is to overcome his psychological problem. Thus, he can choose from a selection of more healthy response options and act against his unhealthy behavioural tendencies. Table 1.1 outlines both self-defeating action tendencies and those associated with more healthy functioning. The ability to act against our action tendencies is, as we shall see, central to our understanding of the REBT theory of therapeutic change.

The ABCDEs of REBT

You are now in a position to understand what has been called the ABCDEs of REBT. You will find this formulation in virtually every book that has been published on REBT, so you need to become very familiar with it.

A

A stands for activating event. When considering one of your client's emotional episodes, you are looking for the aspect of the activating event that triggered the client's irrational belief at B (below). Following the lead of Don Beal (personal communication) I call this the critical A. Critical As can be actual events, but are more likely to be inferences.

B

B stands for your client's rational and irrational beliefs which, as discussed on p. 4, are evaluative in nature. I have also presented the four major types of rational and irrational beliefs as they are featured in REBT (see pp. 4–8). While some REBT therapists prefer to place all cognitive activity under B, it is my practice to put only rational and irrational beliefs under B and to place other cognitions (e.g. inferences) at A.

C

C stands for the person's emotional and/or behavioural response to the beliefs that he holds about the event (or inference) in question. Table 1.1 is relevant here in that it outlines the REBT view of the difference between healthy negative emotions and their unhealthy counterparts. It is easy to forget that C also stands for a behavioural response. Sometimes your client will exhibit self-defeating behaviour based on a set of irrational beliefs he holds about a critical A. When this occurs, either the behaviour occurs without corresponding emotion or it is designed to 'ward off' your client's disturbed feelings.

D

D stands for disputing. In particular, it stands for disputing your client's irrational beliefs by asking questions that encourage the person to question the empirical, logical and pragmatic status of her irrational beliefs.

E

E stands for the effects of disputing. When disputing is successful it helps the client to change her feelings and actions at C because she has changed her thinking at B. In addition, when disputing is successful, it helps the person to make more functional inferences at A.

Having spelled out the ABCDEs of REBT, I will briefly show how some of these interact in complex ways (see Chapter 5 for a full discussion of this issue).

The Principle of Psychological Interactionism

So far, you could be forgiven if you thought that REBT considers that thinking, feeling and behaviour are separate psychological systems. However, this is far from the case. When Albert Ellis originated REBT in the mid-1950s, he put forward the view that thinking (including imagery), feeling and behaviour are interdependent, interacting psychological processes.

Thus, when a person experiences an emotion at C, he has the tendency to think (A and B) and act in a certain way (as shown in Table 1.1). Also when someone holds a rational or irrational belief (at B) about a negative event (at A), this will influence his feelings and behaviours (at C). Finally, if a person acts in a certain way, this will be related to his feelings and thoughts.

What follows from this is that REBT therapists need to pay close attention to thoughts, feelings and behaviour in the assessment process, and that they need to use a variety of cognitive, emotive and behavioural techniques in the intervention phase of therapy.

The Process of Therapeutic Change

In order to practise brief REBT effectively, it is important to have an understanding of the process of therapeutic change. This knowledge will help you to use REBT interventions in the most relevant sequence. I will briefly mention the steps that clients need to take in REBT to experience therapeutic change, before discussing each step in greater detail. While I put these steps in a certain order, please note that this order is flexible and should certainly not be applied rigidly in therapy. Also, although I will not mention them here, there will be problems along the way since therapeutic change is rarely, if ever, a smooth process. After these two caveats, here are the steps:

- understanding the principles of emotional responsibility;
- understanding the determinants of one's psychological problems;
- setting goals and committing oneself to achieving them;
- understanding and committing oneself to the REBT means of achieving one's goals;
- putting this learning into practice;
- maintaining these gains.

UNDERSTANDING THE PRINCIPLES OF EMOTIONAL RESPONSIBILITY

I discussed these principles at length at the beginning of this chapter. Of the two principles of emotional responsibility discussed above, it is the *specific* principle of emotional responsibility that clients need to learn, since this principle outlines the REBT view of psychological disturbance and health. Secondly, if clients do not grasp or do not accept this principle, then they will derive little benefit from REBT.

UNDERSTANDING THE DETERMINANTS OF ONE'S PSYCHOLOGICAL PROBLEMS

This step concerns therapist and client pooling resources to apply the specific principle of emotional responsibility to illuminate the determinants of the client's emotional problems. It involves the therapist helping the client to specify and give examples of these problems so that these can be assessed. Assessment is directed towards identifying unhealthy emotions, the actual or inferred events that provide the context for these emotions, the behaviours that the client enacts when she is experiencing her unhealthy emotions and, most importantly, the irrational beliefs that lie at the core of the client's problems. Unless the client understands the determinants of her problems and agrees with this assessment, REBT will falter at this point.

SETTING GOALS AND COMMITTING ONESELF TO
ACHIEVING THEM

An important part of therapeutic change is setting goals and committing time, energy and effort to taking the necessary steps to achieving them. Let us consider each of these points in turn.

Goal-setting

There is an old adage: 'If you don't know where you're going, you won't know when you've got there.' This points to the importance of setting goals in the therapeutic change process. This is particularly important in brief therapy. If you have a short period of time with a client then if you both know where the client is going, you can tailor the therapeutic work to helping the client achieve his goals. Bordin (1979) noted that agreement on therapeutic goals is an important ingredient and one part of a tripartite view of the working alliance that has gained much prominence in psychotherapy research (Horvath and Greenberg, 1994). Many people have outlined the nature of the client's goals that it is important to negotiate. In brief REBT you should help your clients to set goals which are specific, realistic, achievable, measurable and which aid their overall psychological well-being. Your clients should 'own' their goals, which means that they should set them primarily for their own well-being and not to please anybody else (e.g. significant others or you as therapist).

However, as an REBT therapist you have an important goal for your clients and you must be open about this and discuss it frankly with them. This goal is that your clients learn and practise the skills of what might be called REBT self-help therapy so that they can use them after brief therapy has finished. Indeed, this book is based on the idea that in brief REBT your role is to give away to your clients as much of REBT as they are able to learn. You will, of course, have to help your clients understand that learning these skills will help them to achieve their therapeutic goals, otherwise they will have little interest in learning them. As Bordin (1979) noted, helping your clients to see the relevance of your and their therapeutic tasks to achieving their goals is a central part of the process of brief REBT. Not all clients will want to learn these self-help skills and you can help them (albeit less effectively) without teaching them these skills. However, if you don't offer your clients this opportunity, they will certainly not be able to take advantage of it!

Making a Commitment to Achieve Goals

Goal-setting will be an academic exercise unless your clients are prepared to commit themselves to achieving the goals. A major reason why people do not keep to their new year resolutions for very long is that they are not prepared to do what is necessary to achieve what they have resolved. They want the gain without the pain. So as part of the goal-setting process, discuss with your clients how much time, effort and energy they will have to expend in order to achieve their goals. Then ask them if they are willing to make such an investment. If they are, then you may wish to make a formal agreement with them to this effect. If they are not prepared to make the necessary investment, then you will have to set new goals in line with the kinds of investment they are prepared to make. Of course, this may all change once your work with your client has advanced. Nevertheless, it is important to get brief REBT off on the right foot in this respect. So, in short, set goals with your clients that they are prepared to commit to before you do any further therapy work with them.

UNDERSTANDING AND COMMITTING TO THE REBT MEANS
OF ACHIEVING ONE'S GOALS

After you have agreed on these goals you then have to ensure that your client understands your suggestions concerning how these goals can best be reached. This is the aspect of brief REBT where the technical nature of the therapy comes to the fore. REBT does have definite suggestions concerning what clients need to do in order to achieve their goals. These suggestions take the form of specific techniques (see Ellis and Dryden, 1987, for a description of some of the more important of these techniques). In order for clients to understand the nature of REBT, you need to be able to explain what you are going to do in therapy and what is expected of your client in ways that are clear and detailed. You want clients to proceed with therapy having made an informed decision about REBT. In your description you need to stress two things: you need to show your client how putting into practice the technical aspects of the therapy will help her to achieve her goals; and you need to explain what investments of time, energy and effort your client needs to make in putting REBT techniques into practice.

I have found it very useful at this juncture to point out to clients that there exist other approaches to therapy and that if what I have to offer doesn't make sense to them, if a client doesn't think that REBT will be helpful to her or if she thinks it requires too much of an investment for her, then I suggest other treatment possibilities, discuss these with the client and make a judicious referral.

PUTTING THIS LEARNING INTO PRACTICE

It is not sufficient for clients to understand that they have to put REBT techniques into practice, nor even to commit themselves to so doing. They actually have to do it. Otherwise they will have 'intellectual insight', which in this context may be seen as a light and occasionally held conviction that their irrational beliefs are irrational and their rational beliefs are rational. While gaining this 'intellectual insight' is important, it is insufficient to help clients to achieve their goals. For this to occur, clients need a fair measure of what might be called 'emotional insight', which in this context is the same realization about rational and irrational beliefs as in intellectual insight, but one which is strongly and frequently held. It is this emotional insight which affects a person's feelings and influences his behaviour, and this is the true goal of clients' putting their learning into practice in their everyday lives.

There are several dimensions of between-session practice that are important.

Repetition

It is important for clients to go over new rational beliefs many times before they begin to believe them. This repetition applies to the use of cognitive, emotive and behavioural techniques.

Force and Energy

One useful way that clients can move from intellectual insight to emotional insight is to employ techniques with force and energy. However, it is important that they can understand and see the relevance of particular beliefs rationally before forcefully and energetically working to internalize them.

Vividness

The use of what I have called vivid techniques in REBT (Dryden, 1986) can help clients to bring to mind their rational beliefs more than standard, non-vivid techniques. Vividness tends to increase the impact of rational concepts and thus makes it easier for clients to retrieve them from memory at times when it is necessary for them to do so. As such, they will get more practice at thinking rationally than they would ordinarily do.

It is important for REBT therapists to take great care when they negotiate homework assignments with their clients and this is particularly true in brief therapy, where it is crucial to help clients make effective use of therapeutic time. However, no matter how much care you take when negotiating such assignments, your clients may still have difficulty putting them into practice. It is important to help them to identify and overcome such obstacles.

MAINTAINING THERAPEUTIC GAINS

Once your clients have achieved their goals, this is not the end of the therapeutic story, although many of your clients will think or hope that it is. If they have such thoughts and hopes then they will stop using the principles that you have taught them and increase the chance that they will experience a lapse or, more seriously, a relapse. I define a lapse as a minor return to the problem state, while a relapse is a major return to this state. If your clients are to maintain their therapeutic gains they have to be helped to do so and take responsibility for this maintenance work themselves. This involves relapse prevention and spreading the effect of change.

Relapse Prevention

It is important to deal with relapse prevention before the end of REBT, otherwise the client may not be prepared for the re-emergence of his problems. It is rare for clients not to experience lapses and if they do they need prior help to deal with a lapse when it occurs. If a lapse, or a series of lapses, is not dealt with it may lead to a relapse, since relapses tend to occur when lapses are not identified and dealt with by the person concerned.

Relapse prevention involves the following steps:

(1) Recognizing that lapses are likely to occur and thinking rationally about this point; (2) identifying the likely contexts in which lapses are likely to occur and problem-solving each salient element; (3) exposing oneself to the problematic contexts and using the problem-solving skills previously learned to prevent the development of the lapse; (4) committing oneself to continuing this process for as long as necessary.

If the worst comes to the worst and a relapse does occur then you should help your client to think rationally about this grim reality. Understanding of how this developed should be sought before further treatment decisions are made.

If it looks unlikely that your client will achieve her therapeutic goals by the end of therapy, it is still worth raising the issue of relapse prevention, although this will have to be done rather cursorily; a written handout on relapse prevention supplementing your verbal explanation is useful here. You will need to do this after you have helped your client to formulate a plan which she can follow to achieve her goals after therapy has formally ended.

SPREADING THE EFFECT OF CHANGE

Another important way of helping to ensure that your client maintains his gains is to encourage him to generalize what he has learned about overcoming his problems in certain contexts to other contexts. Thus, if a client has overcome his fear of refusing unreasonable requests at work and is now asserting himself when relevant, he can take what he has learned to enable him to do this and use it to help him to say no when his parents and parents-in-law make unreasonable requests of him in his personal life. The more clients can spread the effect of change in this way the more they will maintain and even enhance their therapy gains.

Final Word

This introduction to some of the important theoretical and practical principles of REBT has necessarily been brief. For an extended review of the theory that underpins REBT, I suggest that you consult my book *Invitation to Rational-Emotive Psychology* (Dryden, 1994). For a comprehensive overview of how to practise REBT in a variety of treatment modalities, I recommend a book that I wrote with Albert Ellis: *The Practice of Rational-Emotive Therapy* (Ellis and Dryden, 1987).

References

Beck, A.T. (1976) *Cognitive Therapy and the Emotional Disorders.* New York: International Universities Press.

Bordin, E.S. (1979) 'The generalizability of the psychoanalytic concept of the working alliance', *Psychotherapy: Theory, Research and Practice*, 16: 252–60.

Dryden, W. (1986) 'Vivid RET', in A. Ellis and R. Grieger (eds), *Handbook of Rational-Emotive Therapy*, Volume 2. New York: Springer.

Dryden, W. (1994) *Invitation to Rational-Emotive Psychology.* London: Whurr.

Dryden, W. (1995) *Preparing for Client Change in Rational Emotive Behaviour Therapy.* London: Whurr.

Ellis, A. (1994) *Reason and Emotion in Psychotherapy*, revised and expanded edn. New York: Birch Lane Press.

Ellis, A. and Dryden, W. (1987) *The Practice of Rational-Emotive Therapy*. New York: Springer.

Horvath, A. and Greenberg, L. (eds) (1994) *The Working Alliance: Theory, Research and Practice*. New York: Wiley.

Wessler, R.A. and Wessler, R.L. (1980) *The Principles and Practice of Rational-Emotive Therapy*. San Francisco: Jossey-Bass.

2

Reason and Emotion in
Psychotherapy: Thirty Years On

Albert Ellis founded rational emotive behaviour therapy (REBT) in 1955. His influence in the field of psychology is now such that in a survey of the American Psychological Association's clinical and counselling psychologists, published in 1982 (Smith, 1982), he was rated the second most influential psychotherapist (behind Carl Rogers, but ahead of Sigmund Freud). In another study (Heesacker et al., 1982), he was the most cited contributor of works published since 1957 in three major counselling journals over a 27-year period, and a recent study of Canadian clinical psychologists showed that Ellis was their most influential psychotherapist, followed by Carl Rogers and Aaron Beck (Warner, 1991).

Reason and Emotion in Psychotherapy was Albert Ellis's first published book on REBT as a system of psychotherapy. It appeared in 1962 and is still the most frequently cited reference on REBT. Actually, the book is a collection of previously published papers and although Ellis worked on these papers to enable them to be published in book form, the text lacks the coherence of a work prepared especially for publication. Nevertheless, it is still recognized as a classic (Heesacker et al., 1982) and 30 years after its first publication merits detailed study. While many central features of REBT theory presented in Ellis's book remain in place today, it is in the nature of the theory that it encourages flexibility. This quality has permitted a good deal of revision of the 1962 ideas – developments which have cleared up ambiguities and emphasized aspects of REBT which Ellis only alluded to in 1962. This chapter examines some major ideas presented 30 years ago, and points out developments which have modified and extended the theory of REBT and its therapeutic applications.

This chapter was originally presented as an Inaugural Lecture at Goldsmiths College, University of London, on 8 December 1992 and published in the *Journal of Rational-Emotive & Cognitive Behavior Therapy*, 1994, 12(2): 83–99.

Rationality

In 1962, Ellis defined his theory's central tenet of rationality. He said that 'rational' means that which aids and abets human happiness, is consistent with reality, and is logical. Rational thinking, therefore, tends greatly to minimize emotional disturbance. In 1962, Ellis also set out how rational emotive behaviour theory views emotional disturbance. He said that emotional disturbance results when individuals acquire and re-indoctrinate themselves with illogical, inconsistent and unworkable values. These three criteria of rationality and irrationality and their implications for human emotional disturbance remain current and basically unchanged since 1962, although a fourth – flexibility vs. rigidity – has now come to the fore.

Humanistic-Existential Emphasis

Besides the well-known cognitive-behavioural roots of REBT, a humanistic-existential view is found in its concept of humans. REBT sees humans as neither superhuman nor subhuman, and it considers all people equal in their humanity. While REBT believes that biological and, to a lesser extent, social forces determine our psychological make-up, it argues that we retain much free will and choice in forming our emotional well-being. Moreover, we can increase our emotional health and happiness by adopting a policy of long-range hedonism. Long-range hedonists make decisions and act to increase their happiness over time. Short-range hedonists, on the other hand, strive for immediate happiness and gratification, opting to satisfy current frustrations at the probable expense of achieving future and longer-term happiness. Of these humanistic-existential foundations of REBT, all are to be found in the 1962 text, with particular emphasis being placed on the importance of striving for long-range hedonism. Today, the humanistic-existential roots of REBT are more prominent and better integrated with its cognitive-behavioural features than hitherto.

Psychological Interactionism

In 1962, Ellis noted that psychological processes such as cognition, behaviour and emotion are interrelated. This hypothesized interaction remains current in REBT's understanding of human psychological functioning, although the complexity of relationships among these processes and their interaction with the environment is more to the fore now than it was 30 years ago (Ellis, 1991).

Frequently, people wrongly claim that REBT maintains that

cognitions cause emotions. This linear relationship, however, belies the complexity of the cognition–emotion interface, and REBT has never considered it valid. Instead, certain cognitions and emotions are deemed in REBT to overlap and are interrelated in such a complex manner that they become practically indistinguishable from each other.

In 1962, Ellis differentiated between cognitions which are calm, dispassionate appraisals of events, and those which are uncalm, strong, evaluative appraisals of events. The latter are called emotions. REBT theory still considers this distinction applicable, but more modern terms are now used. Thus calm, dispassionate appraisals of events are called cold cognitions, and uncalm, strong, evaluative appraisals of events are now termed hot cognitions. The concepts remain the same, but the descriptive terms are different. This distinction helps us to understand more clearly that it is hot cognitions which significantly overlap with emotional experiences.

Having made the point that from the outset Ellis stressed the interrelatedness of cognition, emotion and behaviour, it is also true that he has always stressed the central role of cognitive processes in this trinity. To quote one of my students, Michael Neenan: 'in REBT theory, cognition is often *primus inter pares* – first amongst equals – in this holy trinity'.

The Role of Evaluative Thinking

One of the most significant changes in REBT theory over the last 30 years clarified what type of belief is at the core of emotional experiences. In 1962, Ellis stated that a person's attitudes, interpretations of events, or what events mean to them, largely determine emotions. Note how general these cognitions are. As we shall see, Ellis is now much more precise about the type of cognition that is involved in emotions. In addition, he occasionally mentioned in the 1962 book that situations or events themselves could directly determine emotions (e.g. 'Married neurotics . . . tend to get upset by their mates' errors and stupidities': Ellis, 1962: 208). Given that Ellis was vague about the types of cognition which are centrally implicated in emotion and given that he sometimes implied that cognitions are not important at all in determining emotion (i.e. by stating that situations or events can directly upset people), the reader of the 1962 book is bound to be confused about the precise determinants of emotional experiences. Readers of REBT texts today are not likely to be confused by such contradictions.

Today, REBT sees situations and a person's interpretations of events as less important in determining emotions than a person's *evaluative* beliefs. These evaluative beliefs are the hot cognitions discussed above. Ellis defines evaluations as judgements or appraisals about interpretations. So, for example, Mary says something unflattering about Jane, and Jane interprets this comment as insulting and becomes angry. According to current REBT theory, Mary's comment does not cause Jane to become angry. Likewise, Jane's interpretation of Mary's comment, as insulting, does not cause her to become angry. Rather, Jane's evaluation of Mary's comment is the cognition that most clearly accounts for her anger. Jane's anger-producing evaluation probably goes something like this: 'Mary absolutely must not say those things about me, and it is awful that she does. Further, her comments prove what a horrible person she is.'

REBT now differentiates between different types of thinking, or cognition. Current theory takes Ellis's original description of how people's cognitions determine their emotions, and further specifies it by dividing these cognitions into three levels (Wessler and Wessler, 1980). At the first level, descriptions occur. Here, for example, Jane notices that Mary spoke words and directed these words towards her. This type of cognition represents the descriptive level in that Jane only notes, or records, what occurs. At the second level of cognition, people make inferences about their recorded descriptions. For example, Jane determines what Mary's words mean about her (i.e. they are insulting). Note that up to now, REBT hypotheses that this inferred insult does not fully explain Jane's anger. Her anger occurs at the third and final level of cognition called the evaluative level. At this level, Jane evaluates her inference of Mary's comment. She decides where it is positive, negative or neutral, and, as we shall see later, appraises the information flexibly or rigidly. So, compared to 1962, REBT theory now more specifically delineates the cognitive processes which are involved in people's disturbances and keenly discriminates evaluations from inferences and descriptions. It also stresses the central role that evaluations play in colouring the inferences which people make about themselves, other people and the world (e.g. Dryden et al., 1989).

Ellis describes this process from inference to evaluation to emotion as the ABCs of REBT. In this model, A stands for an event or a person's inference of that event, and the evaluation of this A occurs at B. A person's B, or evaluative belief, represents his or her judgement or appraisal of A. B then leads to C, which stands for the emotional and behavioural consequences of holding the evaluative belief. Again, REBT theory now places much more emphasis on the complex interactions of A, B and C than it did in 1962 (Ellis, 1991) – see Chapter 5.

Ego Disturbance and Low Frustration Tolerance

Current REBT theory distinguishes between two types of emotional disturbance and notes that these different types commonly interact. In 1962, Ellis noted that global, negative evaluations of the self lead to emotional disturbance. He later called this ego disturbance. Now, he and other REBT therapists argue that an additional, central component of emotional disturbance exists, called low frustration tolerance (LFT). People with a philosophy of LFT make themselves disturbed, for example by believing that they cannot stand or bear frustration. They frequently sabotage their progress in therapy by not working to change themselves because they believe that such work is 'too hard'. A philosophy of LFT basically describes emotionally disturbing beliefs related to undesirable life conditions. Ego disturbance alone could not explain this area of emotional disturbance. The concept of LFT allows REBT to account for a much broader range of emotional disturbance than it could with ego disturbance alone. In 1962, the concept of LFT was mentioned only once (Ellis, 1962: 419) and an alternative term 'I can't stand it' also appears only once – 'Oh my Lord! How terrible this situation is . . . I positively cannot stand it!' (Ellis, 1962: 76). LFT (or discomfort disturbance, to give it its other name) has a central role in REBT's current theory of psychological disturbance and this marks a significant development since the publication of *Reason and Emotion in Psychotherapy*.

Throughout this chapter I have noted that beliefs determine emotional health. What do these beliefs contain, however, which lead to people making themselves emotionally disturbed? Ellis now states that evaluations lead to disturbed negative emotions particularly when they contain a must, and that these musts lie at the core of emotional disturbance. Musts are unconditional, dogmatic, absolutistic demands that the universe obey one's proclamations. They designate statements in which preferences and desires are transmuted into rigid commands which must, have to and absolutely should occur. Evaluative beliefs that are not rigid are preferential in nature and do not contribute to emotional distress, although they may lead to healthy negative feelings when one's desires are not realized, as we shall see later. Preferential evaluative beliefs also promote constructive behaviour leading to fulfilment of one's goals. REBT currently states, therefore, that preferential evaluative beliefs maintain and promote emotional health. Changing these preferences into musts results, however, in emotional disturbance. While this view appeared in embryonic form 30 years ago, it is at the core of REBT theory today.

In 1962 Ellis used the term 'should' much more frequently than the term 'must' to exemplify irrational beliefs, while the converse is true today. The reason for this shift concerns the fact that 'should' has several different meanings while 'must' clearly points to rigidity and demandingness. The word 'should' can mean 'preferably should', 'empirically should' or 'ideally should'; moreover, it can represent a recommendation and it can also point to demandingness. As Ellis saw more clearly that the essence of emotional disturbance was absolutism, rigidity and demandingness, he increasingly used the term 'must' and decreasingly employed the term 'should' to represent this essence.

Awfulizing

In 1962 Ellis hypothesized a process known as awfulizing as a major cognitive determinant of emotional disturbance, and references to this process in *Reason and Emotion in Psychotherapy* are more frequent than references to the role of musts in such disturbance. However, it is probably true that in 1962 Ellis maintained that musts and awfulizing have an equal role in explaining emotional disturbance. Sentences such as: 'I must be liked by everyone', and 'It would be awful if everyone does not like me' would have been seen by Ellis in 1962 as containing the same amount of power to produce emotional disturbance. Today, however, REBT maintains that musts are primary in their ability to effect emotional disturbance and stemming from this 'musturbatory' philosophy are secondary processes which people use to draw conclusions about themselves, other people and their lives. Ellis labelled the first conclusion or derivative as awfulizing although he did not clearly define it in 1962. Currently, awfulizing refers to evaluating an event as more than 100 per cent bad – a magical and grossly exaggerated conclusion based on the musturbatory belief 'This must not be as bad as it is.' This distinction between musts and awfulizing provides a precise and clear theoretical delineation of the nature of psychological disturbance which did not exist 30 years ago.

Ellis used the term awfulizing less frequently than the word catastrophizing in 1962. In fact, he saw awfulizing and catastrophizing as synonyms then. Today, however, REBT therapists argue that human tragedies and catastrophes certainly exist. Just because they exist, however, does not require that people label them as awful. If they do, people make the unrealistic, illogical and self-defeating claim that something which does exist absolutely must not exist. This self-defeating change from a preference to a must leads to emotional disturbance rather than just intense, non-disturbed unhappiness over catastrophic situations.

Self-rating vs. Self-acceptance

Most psychological models of personality propose a model of the self, and attempt to show how disturbances in one's view of one's 'self' lead to emotional disturbance. REBT put forth its model of the self 30 years ago, and it remains virtually unchanged today, although this view of the self is perhaps more coherent and consistent now than it was then. For the last 30 years, the primary theme in REBT's model of the self has centred on suspending evaluation of the self. Ellis stated in 1962 that rating people can only yield meaningful information if humans are static, non-changing organisms and then, as today, he argued that people are too complex for a single rating to represent them accurately. REBT sees people as constantly developing organisms who grow and change. One cannot legitimately label something that grows and changes because the label soon misrepresents what it attempts to describe. No label, therefore, can accurately represent humans because they grow and change. Concepts such as self-rating and self-esteem involve the use of such global labels and are thus clearly illegitimate, inhibiting the emotional growth of complex human organisms.

Since 1962 REBT has viewed humans as fallible creatures who, by nature, cannot be perfected. Ellis maintains that people would benefit from accepting themselves as fallible and trying to learn from their mistakes. People who learn from their mistakes decrease the amount of time they disturb themselves and increase the time they involve themselves in constructive emotional problem-solving, thereby leading happier lives. Humans would do well not to expect to prevent all mistakes because as long as people breathe, think and act, they will make mistakes. While rating themselves increases the chances that people will disturb themselves emotionally, rating their traits and behaviours from a position of unconditional self-acceptance helps them to focus on and change aspects of themselves that inhibit self-actualization. As Ellis noted in 1962, people cannot try to be better, but can attempt to act better.

While REBT's view of the self, laid out above, has remained basically unchanged, Ellis later cleared up a major inconsistency present in his 1962 book. There he stated that 'true self respect . . . comes . . . from liking oneself' (Ellis, 1962: 62) and again:

> An individual who has a good ego or true pride does not have to keep protecting himself about the views of others. . . . Generally he *likes*

himself so much that he can be comfortable even when others disapprove his behavior. (Ellis, 1962: 270, emphasis added)

If you like your*self*, however, you are giving yourself a global rating. This smacks of theoretical inconsistency when one remembers that accurate self-ratings are not possible because (a) people are too complex to merit such ratings; and (b) they constantly change. To like your*self* does not make sense according to REBT's view of the ever-changing self, as Ellis himself notes in the 1962 book (pp. 150–1). Saying that you like mastering a task, for example, but can accept yourself whether or not you master it, more closely describes a healthy view of the self and its vicissitudes. For current REBT theory believes that deriving enjoyment from mastering a valued task will increase a human's chance of being happy. If people enjoy mastering a task, this does not mean that they have to like them*selves*. Rather, it means they rate their acts and through making such ratings can strive to improve their behaviour so that they can maximize happiness and minimize pain. Thus, rating aspects of ourselves is healthy but rating our 'self' is not. This clarification makes REBT's current view of the self more coherent and consistent.

Psychological Health

Much of this chapter considers factors which lead to emotional disturbance, yet it is worth enquiring about REBT's view of factors associated with emotional health. In 1962 Ellis delineated several criteria for psychological health. He stated that an emotionally healthy person demonstrates a healthy and enlightened self- and social interest, a commitment to creative pursuits and an adherence to long-range hedonism. Ellis has added to this list of four criteria. At present the list additionally includes: self-direction, high frustration tolerance, flexibility, acceptance of uncertainty, scientific thinking, acceptance of self as a fallible human being, ability to take calculated risks, holding a non-utopian view of life, and taking responsibility for one's own emotional destiny. Ellis's expansion of his original criteria for psychological health reflects REBT's commitment to extending the explanatory power of its theory.

Healthy and Unhealthy Negative Emotions

Many people seeking psychotherapy wish to get rid of their negative emotions. Current REBT theory does not advocate, however, extinguishing all negative emotions, for REBT now distinguishes between two types of negative emotion: healthy and unhealthy ones.

Ridding the client of unhealthy negative emotions rather than all negative emotions is a paramount goal in REBT. Helping the client to identify and accept healthy negative emotions also becomes a goal during REBT. Briefly, unhealthy negative emotions result from irrational beliefs, and healthy negative emotions stem from rational beliefs. Examples of unhealthy negative emotions include anxiety, depression, shame and demanding anger, while their healthy equivalents are concern, sadness, regret and non-demanding anger (or annoyance). In REBT, counsellors encourage clients to feel healthy negative emotions such as concern when facing adversity. Emotions such as these serve as signals to people that they are in a situation they would do well to change. Healthy negative emotions act, therefore, as behavioural prompts and motivators to encourage people to maximize their happiness and minimize hassles. Ellis did not clearly distinguish between these two types of negative emotion in 1962. Today, this distinction represents a more sophisticated account of negative emotions and provides therapists and clients with a guide as to which type of emotions to minimize, and which type to promote for profitable psychological adjustment and change to occur.

Acquisition and Perpetuation of Psychological Disturbance

Any useful theory of psychological therapy is able to provide an account of how people acquire and perpetuate emotional disturbance. Ellis stated in 1962 that situations can play a large part in how people acquire psychological problems. In several places Ellis indicated that people can be taught to be emotionally disturbed. For example, in talking to a client, Ellis says 'You thought you would be terribly hurt by a girl rejecting you merely because you were *taught* that you would be' (1962: 256) and 'so you were taught that being rejected is awful, frightful' (1962: 257).

Today, Ellis would tell this client that he brought his ability to disturb himself to these teachings and was not made disturbed by the teachings themselves. Indeed, a close reading of the book indicates that Ellis, at the time he wrote *Reason and Emotion in Psychotherapy*, was much more influenced by psychoanalytic thought than he is today. Thus in working with a client called Caleb, Ellis (1962) showed him 'the connection between his psychosomatic symptoms and his father's stroke' and related 'his symptoms to his mother's tendency to baby him when was physically ill and to his dislike of having to take over his father's factory instead of pursuing his own chosen career' (p. 206). Ellis would now pour scorn on such psychoanalytically oriented interpretations.

Today, REBT states that people bring their innate tendency to disturb themselves to events and are not passively made disturbed by events. Parents and culture teach children which superstitions and prejudices to hold. They do not, however, create children's original tendency to unhelpful ritualism, spiritualism and dogmatism. Instead, Ellis maintains that children are *born* with these disturbance-creating tendencies. Today, REBT adheres to the principle of constructivism which describes the idea that people create their own emotional disturbances (Ellis, 1990). Constructivism explains why Ellis has never articulated any elaborate theory of how such disturbances are acquired. For experiences do not directly lead to disturbance; rather people bring their biologically oriented demands to their experiences and disturb themselves emotionally in the process.

Current REBT theory places more emphasis on a biological explanation for human disturbance than on an environmental one. In fact, Ellis maintains now that biology accounts for 80 per cent of psychological disturbance, while environmental factors contribute only 20 per cent (Ellis, 1978). In 1962 Ellis did not attempt to distribute the variance in this way. While the biological emphasis in REBT theory was present 30 years ago, it is now more pronounced, and an important paper published in 1976 showed Ellis's still current view on the extent to which biology influences acquisition of psychological disturbance.

REBT clearly regards biology, then, as the major factor in producing emotional disturbance. Ellis, however, gives people primary control of their emotional reins in *perpetuating* this disturbance. To this day, and since its inception, REBT maintains that people perpetuate their psychological disturbance because they lack three major insights concerning the nature of their problems. Insight number one states that unfortunate situational factors do not determine unhealthy negative emotions. Rather, absolutistic, musturbatory evaluations of situations lead to emotional disturbance.

People may have insight number one, but will still disturb themselves if they do not hold insight number two. This second insight maintains that people perpetuate their absolutistic beliefs by re-indoctrinating themselves with them in the present. Thus, a person may have disturbed himself in the past over some event. However, if he is still disturbed about it, it is because he is currently adhering to a set of irrational beliefs about the past occurrence.

While people may have insights numbers one and two, they will still disturb themselves if they lack insight number three. This final insight requires people to acknowledge that they must actively and repeatedly challenge and dispute their dogmatic beliefs if they are to overcome their emotional and behavioural problems. Unless people take up the Protestant work ethic and work, work and work at challenging and changing their irrational beliefs using cognitive, behavioural and emotive methods, they will continue to disturb themselves.

REBT has always noted that people are not only highly adept at perpetuating their primary problems, but are also extraordinarily skilled at constructing secondary problems about their original problems. Ellis now places more emphasis on this disturbance-perpetuating factor than he did in 1962. An example of this factor occurs when clients make themselves anxious about their primary anxieties. Some people are even more talented at disturbing themselves. Thus, occasionally clients not only come up with secondary problems, but also with tertiary problems (further problems about their secondary problems). For instance, a client came in because he was shoplifting (problem 1). He was also ashamed of his shoplifting (problem 2), and ashamed that he had to seek therapy over it (problem 3). In addition, he berated himself for not working as hard as he believed he must to overcome his original problem (problem 4). While in 1962 Ellis alluded to clients' ability to disturb themselves about their original disturbances, this is given far more prominence in current REBT theory and practice.

Since 1962 Ellis has identified other ways that humans perpetuate their psychological disorders. For example, REBT therapists often ask clients to perform behaviours they are not used to (such as to act differently based on a newly acquired rational philosophy). Clients often report they cannot do these requested behaviours because they 'feel like a phoney' or 'I'm not like that, it's just not me'. Some clients find it difficult to accept that it takes time for a person to grow accustomed to any 'new' behaviour. Due to this, they do not perform the new, more constructive behaviour. Their refusal to feel like a 'phoney' for a while, of course, perpetuates their problem.

Ellis also currently states that self-fulfilling prophecies serve to perpetuate emotional disorders. For instance, an anxious person believes that she will make a fool of herself at a dance where she wishes to meet people. Due to her anxiety about acting foolishly, her thoughts freeze, she does not speak thoughtfully, and ends up actually acting foolishly. Needless to say, this serves to increase her anxiety because she then condemns herself for her foolish act. The role of self-fulfilling prophecies in the perpetuation process was not mentioned by Ellis in his 1962 book.

Finally, Ellis currently states that a philosophy of low frustration tolerance (LFT) perpetuates emotional disturbance. This philosophy was not emphasized in 1962. As mentioned earlier, people with a philosophy of LFT demand that change must not be 'too hard' for them. Change requires, however, very hard work on the part of clients. Due to this requirement, people with LFT do not readily or easily change. They, thus, perpetuate their psychological problems by refusing to do the work necessary to overcome them.

The addition of LFT, self-fulfilling prophecies, and the role of phoney feelings to the list of factors preventing change more fully develops REBT's theory of the perpetuation process. In addition, awareness of these factors further assists clinicians and clients to anticipate and attack directly these problem-causing irrational beliefs in therapy.

Therapeutic Change

In addition to providing an account of how psychological problems are acquired and maintained, a useful theory of therapy needs to account for therapeutic change. Currently, Ellis delineates various levels of therapeutic change which he did not articulate as comprehensively in 1962. He now distinguishes between philosophic (or evaluative) change, inferential change and behavioural change (Dryden and Ellis, 1988). In therapy, Ellis strives to promote philosophic change in clients whenever possible. Achieving profound philosophic change (sometimes called elegant change), requires clients to focus on their dogmatic or musturbatory ideas and to work steadily to change these beliefs to non-dogmatic preferences.

Ellis described another type of change, known as inferential change, which occurs when people alter their inferences about their experiences rather than their evaluations of these experiences. An example of inferential change occurs when a person decides, for example, that someone whom she thought was against her is, in fact, not against her. Rather, she concludes that the person concerned is either neutral towards her or, in fact, on her side.

Lastly, Ellis states that people can change their behaviour. Behavioural change often serves to alter the activating event – i.e. the A part of the ABC model. Dryden and Ellis (1988) maintain that achieving philosophic change frequently leads to inferential and behavioural change, whereas inferential and behavioural change less frequently lead to philosophic change. This explains why Ellis has always stressed the importance of trying to achieve philosophic change.

Ellis did not differentiate these levels of change in his 1962 book.

Rather, he just focused on philosophic change, although he did not call it this. Over the past 30 years, REBT has, in my view, succeeded more than other cognitive-behavioural therapies (CBTs) in outlining how to achieve philosophic change. Other CBTs have mainly concentrated on how to achieve inferential and behavioural change, and have done so quite successfully. In the following comments, I will primarily focus on REBT's pioneering methods of achieving profound philosophic change.

To effect philosophic change, Ellis states that clients first need to realize that they create, to a large degree, their own psychological disturbances. Secondly, they need to recognize fully that they have the ability to change significantly these disturbances. Thirdly, they need to understand that emotional and behavioural disturbances stem largely from irrational, absolutistic beliefs. Fourthly, they need to detect their irrational beliefs and discriminate them from their rational ones. Fifthly, they need to dispute these irrational beliefs using the logical, empirical methods of scientific reasoning. Sixthly, they need to work towards the internalization of their new rational beliefs by employing cognitive, behavioural and emotive methods of change. Finally, they need to continue this process of challenging irrational beliefs and using multi-modal methods of change for the rest of their lives.

While this elaborate process of change can be found in the 1962 book, it appears there in quite a rudimentary form. Some parts of the process, though, did receive heavy emphasis then. For example, in 1962 Ellis stressed the importance of work and practice to effect change as much as he does now. However, other features of the change process that feature now were virtually absent then. Thus, his 1962 book contained only a few cognitive and behavioural change techniques whereas numerous such methods can be found in the current REBT literature (Dryden and Yankura, 1993). In addition, Ellis did not include then any emotive or imaginal techniques which now feature prominently in the REBT therapist's armamentarium. For example, Ellis (1987) now advocates the use of humour as an important emotive technique, whereas the REBT of 1962 seems quite humourless by comparison.

In 1962 Ellis did not discuss many techniques that an REBT therapist could use; he did list, however, those not recommended. These included abreaction, catharsis, dream analysis, free association, interpretation of resistance, analysis of transference, hypnosis, reassurance, reciprocal inhibition, and positive thinking. Ellis still recommends avoiding these techniques. Today, however, some REBT therapists do employ a few of these as well as others derived from alternative therapeutic approaches, without adopting the theory which spawned these techniques. Methods borrowed from other orientations are used in a manner consistent with REBT theory. Likewise, therapists do not employ techniques contra-indicated by the REBT theory. This is an example of what I have called theoretically consistent eclecticism (Dryden, 1987a). In this form of eclecticism, theory guides technique selection, which is not restricted to the limited number of techniques spawned by the theory itself.

The Role of Force and Energy in Change

In 1962, Ellis encouraged people to work, work, work at changing their irrational beliefs. In 1992 he was still encouraging such work. However, he states that people do better when they use force and energy to change their irrational beliefs and behaviours. Thus, Ellis argues that people will challenge their irrational beliefs more successfully by questioning them in a vigorous manner, and by accentuating forcefully more logical, rational beliefs as alternatives. In addition, Ellis recommends that clients expose themselves as fully as they can to their fears. He thus favours the use of flooding rather than the use of gradual desensitization techniques. So, instead of recommending that a social phobic phone one friend per week, he encourages them to phone five. The more recent ideas of force and energy in behaviour change and the use of full *in vivo* exposure clarify a central tenet of REBT and extend its clinical application.

The Therapeutic Relationship

Of course, utilization of any technique takes place within the context of a therapeutic relationship. In this relationship, client and therapist work together to help the client. How the therapist should act in this partnership is addressed in countless volumes in the literature on counselling and psychotherapy. Carl Rogers (1957) has described one of the most enduring and widely accepted models of how a therapist should interact with a client. In his model he outlined a set of necessary and sufficient conditions for therapeutic change. Thirty years ago, Ellis said that Rogers's model was wrong. He maintained that Rogers's core conditions of empathy, respect and genuineness are desirable but neither necessary nor sufficient to effect psychological change. Instead, he stated that a therapist needs to act as a model and teacher to help the client change. Today, REBT therapists place more emphasis on building and maintaining a therapeutic alliance with their clients than they did in 1962 (Dryden, 1987b). The role of the therapist as model and teacher, however, remains unchanged.

Summary

In 1962 REBT displayed important features still current. These include the interrelatedness of cognitive, emotive and behavioural processes, the important role that cognition plays in psychological problems, its humanistic view of the self and the futility and dangers of self-rating. The emphasis on perpetuation rather than acquisition processes of emotional disturbance holds good now as it did then, and the core view of therapeutic change is essentially the same, despite further, more recent elaborations. One can also find the beginnings of a model of psychological health in 1962 that has been more fully developed since that time.

Significant change has occurred in REBT since 1962 that updates several of Ellis's original ideas. These include the distinction between inferences and evaluations, the primacy of musts in accounting for psychological disturbance, the clear distinction between healthy and unhealthy negative emotions and the greater role accorded to force and energy in the change process. Aspects of psychoanalytic theory, as well as conditioning theory, featured in 1962 no longer appear, and a greater emphasis is placed on biological aspects of emotional disturbance now. Finally, a greater range of cognitive, imaginal, emotive and behavioural methods are found in current REBT literature than in *Reason and Emotion in Psychotherapy*, where Ellis restricts himself to illustrating a few cognitive and behavioural techniques.

REBT, then, has grown and developed. In large part, this reflects the theory's flexibility and the competent people who have worked to make REBT one of the most viable and widely used cognitive-behaviour therapies. In these, I modestly include myself.

Note

Since this paper was first published, Ellis (1994) has published a revised and expanded edition of *Reason and Emotion in Psychotherapy*.

References

Dryden, W. (1987a) 'RET as a theoretically consistent form of eclecticism', in W. Dryden, *Current Issues in Rational-Emotive Therapy*. London: Croom Helm.

Dryden, W. (1987b) 'The therapeutic alliance in rational-emotive individual therapy', in W. Dryden, *Current Issues in Rational-Emotive Therapy*. London: Croom Helm.

Dryden, W. and Ellis, A. (1988) 'Rational-emotive therapy', in K.S. Dobson (ed.), *Handbook of Cognitive-Behavioral Therapies*. New York: Guilford.

Dryden, W. and Yankura, J. (1993) *Counselling Individuals: A Rational-Emotive Handbook*, London: Whurr.

Dryden, W., Ferguson, J. and McTeague, S. (1989) 'Beliefs and inferences: a test of a rational-emotive hypothesis. 2: On the prospect of seeing a spider', *Psychological Reports*, 64: 115–23.

Ellis, A. (1962) *Reason and Emotion in Psychotherapy*, New York: Lyle Stuart.

Ellis, A. (1976) 'The biological basis of human irrationality', *Journal of Individual Psychology*, 32: 145–68.

Ellis, A. (1978) 'Toward a theory of personality', in R. Corsini (ed.), *Readings in Current Personality Theories*. Itasca, IL: F.E. Peacock.

Ellis, A. (1987) 'The use of rational humorous songs in psychotherapy', in W.F. Fry Jr and W.A. Salameh (eds), *Handbook of Humor in Psychotherapy: Advances in the Clinical Use of Humor*. Sarasota, FL: Professional Resource Exchange.

Ellis, A. (1990) 'Is rational-emotive therapy (RET) "rationalist" or "constructivist"?', in W. Dryden (ed.), *The Essential Albert Ellis*. New York: Springer.

Ellis, A. (1991) 'The revised ABC's of rational-emotive therapy (RET)', *Journal of Rational-Emotive & Cognitive Behavior Therapy*, 9: 139–72.

Ellis, A. (1994) *Reason and Emotion in Psychotherapy*, revised and expanded edn. New York: Birch Lane Press.

Heesacker, M., Heppner, P.P. and Rogers, M.E. (1982) 'Classics and emerging classics in counseling psychology', *Journal of Counseling Psychology*, 29: 400–5.

Rogers, C.R. (1957) 'The necessary and sufficient conditions of therapeutic personality change', *Journal of Consulting Psychology*, 21: 95–103.

Smith, D. (1982) 'Trends in counseling and psychotherapy', *American Psychologist*, 37: 802–9.

Warner, R.E. (1991) 'A survey of theoretical orientations of Canadian clinical psychologists', *Canadian Psychology*, 32: 525–8.

Wessler, R.A. and Wessler, R.L. (1980) *The Principles and Practice of Rational-Emotive Therapy*, San Francisco: Jossey-Bass.

3

When Musts Are Not Enough

A Note on Determining the Type of Your Client's Disturbance by Referring to Her Secondary Irrational Beliefs

About 15 years ago Albert Ellis introduced the important concept of discomfort anxiety into the REBT literature and distinguished it from ego anxiety (Ellis, 1979, 1980). Later, this concept was broadened to include, amongst others, discomfort depression and today REBT therapists distinguish between discomfort disturbance and ego disturbance.

As is well known, Albert Ellis has long argued that musts are at the core of much psychological disturbance, and that other irrational beliefs (i.e. awfulizing, low frustration tolerance and self/other downing) are derived from these musts (cf. Ellis, 1993). This point has been made humorously by Ellis in the aphorism: 'Shouldhood leads to shithood. You're never a shit without a should.' Following Ellis, musts therefore can be regarded as primary irrational beliefs and awfulizing, LFT and self/other downing can be regarded as secondary irrational beliefs.

Although musts may be primary irrational beliefs, they are in fact insufficient in helping REBT therapists to tell whether a client's problem is an example of ego disturbance, discomfort disturbance or, indeed, both. Let's consider two examples.

The Case of Sybil

Let's first take the case of Sybil. She had the following primary irrational belief: 'I must have the approval of my boss.' Now, my basic thesis is that it is not possible to tell from this primary irrational belief whether Sybil's problem is one of ego, discomfort disturbance or both. To determine this we need to know what her secondary irrational beliefs are. Let's review them:

This chapter is an expansion of an article that was originally published in *The Rational Emotive Behaviour Therapist*, 1994, 2(2): 59–60.

- 'It would be terrible if my boss did not approve of me.'
- 'I couldn't stand it if my boss disapproved of me.'
- 'I would be no good if my boss disapproved of me.'

This final belief shows that one component of Sybil's problem with her boss is ego disturbance. But how can we judge whether there is also a component which points to discomfort disturbance? We can do this by asking her the following question: 'If you were able to accept yourself in the face of your boss's disapproval, would you still believe that it would be terrible if he disapproved of you and would you still believe that you couldn't stand it if he disapproved of you?'

If Carol's reply is 'yes' to one or both of these questions, then her problem has both ego and discomfort disturbance features. However, if her reply is 'no' then her problem is likely to be an example of ego disturbance alone.

Now, let's consider the situation where Sybil has the following set of secondary irrational beliefs:

- 'It would be terrible if my boss did not approve of me.'
- 'I couldn't stand it if my boss disapproved of me.'

However, she believes that she would not put herself down in the face of her boss's approval.

This situation indicates that Sybil's problem is probably an example of discomfort disturbance alone.

The Case of Terry

Now let's consider the case of Terry and introduce the concept of strongly and weakly held beliefs. He held the following musturbatory, irrational belief: 'I must get promoted at work.' Does this belief lead to ego or discomfort disturbance? Again, the only way to answer this question is to inspect the derivatives of his must (i.e. his secondary irrational beliefs). Once you have specified the person's must and its derivatives you have identified what I call the person's full irrational belief.

Thus, if Terry's full irrational belief is 'I must get promoted at work and if I don't it would prove I am an inadequate person', then he is experiencing ego disturbance, when this self-downing belief is stronger than any LFT belief that he might have. On the other hand, if his full irrational belief is 'I must get promoted at work and if I don't my life will be more uncomfortable if I'm not and I couldn't stand this discomfort', then he is experiencing discomfort disturbance, if his LFT belief is stronger than any self-downing belief that he might have. Thus, again, while musts may be primary in a person's disturbance, it is only by identifying the secondary irrational belief derivatives that we can understand the true nature of his disturbance.

Incidentally, the presence of awfulizing beliefs also does not help us to determine whether the person is experiencing ego or discomfort disturbance. Thus, if the person says 'I must get promoted at work and it is awful if I don't', he could mean it is awful because it would mainly prove he would be an inadequate person or because the discomfort of not being promoted would be unbearable. So if clients provide a demanding belief and an awfulizing belief, you still need to identify the presence or absence of an LFT belief and/or a self-downing belief in order to determine whether their problem reflects mainly ego or mainly discomfort disturbance.

Figure 3.1 provides a summary of the points I have made so far. However, a good rule of thumb is this: when a person has a demanding belief, but no associated self-downing belief (or when this belief is quite weak), he is probably experiencing discomfort disturbance. However, if a self-downing belief is present and is stronger than any associated LFT belief, the person is probably experiencing ego disturbance.

EGO DISTURBANCE

Must + self-downing (awfulizing and LFT beliefs may also be present) [self-downing belief is stronger than the LFT belief]

DISCOMFORT DISTURBANCE

Must + LFT belief (awfulizing belief may also be present) [self-downing belief is absent or is weaker than the LFT belief]

NATURE OF DISTURBANCE UNKNOWN

1 Must + awfulizing belief [LFT and self-downing beliefs not assessed]
2 Must + awfulizing belief + LFT belief [self-downing belief not assessed]
3 Must + awfulizing + LFT belief + self-downing belief [strength of LFT and self-downing beliefs not assessed]

Figure 3.1 *Guidelines for determining ego and discomfort disturbance*

Conclusion

As this brief chapter makes clear, if you wish to determine whether your client's problem is an example of ego disturbance, discomfort disturbance or a combination of the two, then you cannot rely on her primary irrational belief alone. Rather, you need to inspect closely the client's secondary irrational beliefs, as illustrated in the example above. While musts might be primary irrational beliefs, a knowledge of your client's secondary irrational beliefs is necessary to gain an accurate understanding of the type of your client's disturbance. In this sense, musts are not enough.

References

Ellis, A. (1979) 'Discomfort anxiety: a new cognitive behavioral construct. Part 1', *Rational Living*, 14(2): 3–8.

Ellis, A. (1980) 'Discomfort anxiety: a new cognitive behavioral construct. Part 2', *Rational Living*, 15(1): 25–30.

Ellis, A. (1993) 'Fundamentals of rational-emotive therapy for the 1990s', in W. Dryden and L.K. Hill (eds), *Innovations in Rational-Emotive Therapy*. Newbury Park, CA: Sage.

4

The Issue of Behaviour in REBT

In the ABC framework that is so central to REBT, C stands for the emotional *and* behavioural consequences of holding evaluative beliefs (B) about A. In most texts on REBT when Cs are discussed, the emphasis is on emotional Cs. In this chapter, I concentrate on behavioural Cs and consider a number of important issues that emerge when we look at the REBT view of behaviour.

Behaviour is Purposive

When a person acts in a certain way, that action can be seen as having a purpose, i.e. through that behaviour the person is seeking to achieve something. The person may not be aware of this purpose, but this does not negate the REBT proposition that much behaviour is purposive. The main purposes of behaviour are:

- to initiate an emotional state;
- to stop an emotional state;
- to avoid an emotional state;
- to reduce the intensity of an emotional state;
- to intensify an emotional state;
- to maintain an emotional state;
- to elicit a response from the physical environment;
- to elicit a response from the interpersonal environment; and
- to act in a way that is consistent with one's values, standards and goals.

I deal with each of these purposes in turn and show when such behaviour stems from irrational beliefs.

PURPOSIVE BEHAVIOUR I: TO INITIATE AN EMOTIONAL
STATE

A person may act to initiate either a positive or a negative emotional state. Let us take the former situation first. When considering

---

This chapter was originally published in W. Dryden, *Invitation to Rational-Emotive Psychology*, London: Whurr, 1994.

the purposes of behaviour, it is important to distinguish between short-term goals and long-term goals. REBT theory posits that we are at our happiest when actively pursuing meaningful and absorbing long-term goals. When we act in the service of these long-term goals, we often have to put up with short-term discomfort. We do so because we think that it is worth it and because we are committed to the idea that our present behaviour will bring long-term happiness. In this important sense behaviour can lead to a projected positive emotional state (see also Purpose IX, pp. 64–6).

Now let me consider behaviour where the purpose is to initiate shorter-term positive emotional states. We are all familiar with the desire to seek out a positive emotional state when feeling bored, for example. Thus, we may actively involve ourselves in an interest so that we may gain a present sense of enjoyment. Also, we may turn to pleasurable immediate diversions, such as playing a favourite cassette tape or reading a novel. These activities are generally healthy for us unless they also serve a different purpose, e.g. helping us to avoid something that we need to face up to (see pp. 55–7).

Conversely, we may pursue enjoyable experiences which are more dangerous. Thus, we may seek out activities which contain a high element of risk, like pot-holing, rock-climbing and paragliding. If we are highly skilled in these activities then we will reduce the risk, but for those who seek thrills, the elements of risk is what makes the activity thrilling. Alternatively, we may take drugs to initiate a highly pleasurable state. The risks of drug-taking are well known and some drugs are so addictive that we may very quickly take them for a different purpose – to get rid of the highly unpleasant emotional state known as withdrawal. Later in this chapter, I discuss behaviour, the purpose of which is to stop an emotional state. When a person engages in behaviour designed to initiate a short-term intensely pleasurable state, but which places that person's well-being in danger, it may be that he holds the following irrational belief: 'I must experience these pleasurable feelings and I can't stand depriving myself of such feelings when they are so readily available to me.'

Behaviour can also have the purpose of initiating a negative emotional state. This may seem to be a strange idea, but the phenomenon does occur in clinical practice. Richard Wessler and Sheenah Hankin-Wessler, two psychotherapists who work in North America, argue that some people behave in a way to provoke a negative feeling in themselves. It is important to stress that this process is not a conscious one. The person does not say to himself: 'I think I will do this because it will lead me to feel bad.' He acts, however, as if this was his motivation. Why should a person act to feel bad? The Wesslers argue that he does so because this negative feeling is familiar to him.

Let me give an example of this phenomenon. Joe, a 27-year-old mature student, has a history of failing courses at college and yet persists at his studies, moving from one subject to another in the hope of succeeding at something. At the time of the incident that I will describe, he was studying drama and was doing very well. It looked as if for the first time in his life Joe would be successful at a college subject. His essay marks were good, his acting skills were first-class; all Joe had to do to achieve his qualification was to hand in a practical log. The long-awaited success was close at hand. Or was it? As you may surmise, Joe found a way to sabotage his success. In this case he developed crippling writer's block. Interestingly, this did not develop until his success was in sight. In therapy, it emerged that although Joe was very uncomfortable with the view that he had about himself, namely that he was a failure, he was also comfortable with this familiar self-view because it enabled him to predict the world with some degree of certitude. The prospect of succeeding, then, led Joe to sabotage his position by developing writer's block. Remember, Joe was not aware of the sabotaging aspect of his behaviour; it occurred outside of his awareness.

As long as there was a chance of passing his course, Joe could not write. He overcame his block only several weeks after it became apparent that once again he had failed. Joe's feelings about yet another failure were mixed. On the one hand and consciously, he was very disappointed to have failed once again. On the other hand, he was secretly relieved that he did not have to confront unfamiliar situations to which his success would have, in his mind, inevitably led. His failure gave him that sense of familiarity that his writer's block was designed to bring about. To put it more graphically, Joe snatched failure from the jaws of success. His behaviour enabled him to feel the familiar, but painful, feelings that were associated with his belief that he was a failure. Of course part of Joe wanted to succeed and this explains why a few months later he enrolled on a different course, destined no doubt to repeat a painful, but familiar script unless he can use his understanding of the dynamics of his situation to bring about a change in his attitude towards himself and thereby stop himself from behaving in a way that initiates a negative emotional state.

As this example shows, behaviour can serve several different purposes simultaneously. Joe's behaviour was not only designed to initiate a negative emotional state, i.e. feelings of failure; it was simultaneously designed to initiate a sense of familiarity which can be regarded as a positive aspect of his overall emotional state. Note that an emotional experience can have both positive and negative aspects. Although behaviour is multi-purposive, I will deal in this chapter with one major purpose at a time.

PURPOSIVE BEHAVIOUR II: TO TERMINATE AN EMOTIONAL
STATE

We may also behave in ways to rid ourselves of emotional states that are negative and positive. Let me consider the cessation of negative states first. When we are bored we may act to end this emotional state. Here, our primary purpose is to stop the boredom rather than to seek pleasure. Again, it is important to distinguish between unpleasantness-ceasing behaviours that are relatively harmless and those that are self-defeating or downright dangerous. I have already mentioned drug-taking as an example of the latter, so let me briefly discuss behaviours, the purpose of which is to dispose of an unpleasant emotional state, but which turn out to be self-defeating for the individual.

A good example of this is when a person leaves a situation when he is anxious. The purpose of this withdrawal is to end the person's anxiety and in this respect it is frequently successful. However, and this point needs to be underscored, such behaviour often leads to greater problems for the individual in the future, in that such withdrawal tends to reinforce the person's irrational beliefs that underpin his anxiety and deprive him of an opportunity of identifying, challenging and eventually changing these beliefs. Let me exemplify these points.

Jim, a 25-year-old insurance clerk, tends to get anxious in social situations. Whenever his anxiety level increases beyond a point that he is prepared to tolerate, he leaves the situation, and excuses himself, claiming that he has a headache or some other minor pain. Jim's anxiety is based primarily on the following irrational belief: 'I must not say anything foolish in public. If I do, it would be awful and would prove what a fool I am.' This belief leads Jim to stay silent much of the time, the purpose of which is to minimize his anxiety – I will discuss this purpose more fully later in this chapter. More importantly, this belief triggers Jim's anxiety when it becomes clear to him that he cannot stay silent any longer. At this point he withdraws from the situation, the purpose of which is to bring Jim's anxiety to an end. When Jim leaves the social situation he implicitly believes the following: 'Oh my God! People are looking at me and they expect me to say something. I have to get away before I make a fool of myself.' As he leaves at this point, he not only reinforces his irrational belief, but he also deprives himself of opportunities of showing himself (1) that while he would prefer it if he did not say something stupid in public, there is no law of the universe that says that he must not do so; and (2) that he is not a fool for saying something foolish in company, but a fallible human being who has said the wrong thing.

A person can also behave in a way to terminate a positive emotional state. Take the example of Wendy, a 34-year-old woman who is studying hard for her professional accountancy exams. One evening she takes a break from her studies to go out with two college friends. She intends to stay out for only a couple of hours but in fact finds herself spending several hours with them. When she focuses on how much she is enjoying herself, she explains that she has to go home and promptly leaves. What is happening here is that when Wendy realizes what a good time she is having, she leaves because she believes that she absolutely should not be enjoying herself at a time when she should be studying. As she believes that she has not earned her enjoyment, she cuts it short.

PURPOSIVE BEHAVIOUR III: TO AVOID AN EMOTIONAL STATE

People frequently act in a way so as to avoid an emotional state. Let us first consider an instance of a person avoiding an unpleasant emotional state. A good example of this would be procrastinating behaviours. While there are several reasons why people procrastinate, here I will deal with one of the major reasons, the avoidance of discomfort. I used to work in a university counselling service and during that time I saw many students who came for help with procrastination. When I asked them why they put off studying, a large number replied that they never seemed to be in the mood. While this by no means fully explains procrastinating behaviour, it is a key dynamic of such behaviour.

According to the present analysis, we can understand procrastination as behaviour whose purpose is partly to help the person avoid experiencing an unpleasant emotional state, in this case discomfort, since these students would initially have felt uncomfortable if they had done something (in this case studying) that they were not in the mood for.

Such avoidance behaviour can come in different guises. Some students would involve themselves in pleasurable diversions. While on the surface it seems as if the purpose of such behaviour is to initiate a pleasurable emotional state, and of course there is that element to it, the main goal of such behaviour was to help the people concerned to avoid the experience of discomfort. Other students would engage in passive avoidance activities, such as sleeping, daydreaming and simply sitting for long periods of time in a chair thinking about getting down to work. Yet other students became engaged in what I call 'pseudo-work'. Here they would involve themselves in activities that could be mistaken for work, but when considered carefully turn out to be avoidance behaviour. Examples of pseudo-work include arranging one's books in order so that one can get easy access to relevant material, tidying one's desk so that one has plenty of space in which to work and ensuring that one's pens are properly filled with ink and one's pencils are properly sharpened.

You may wonder how to judge whether such activities constitute work or pseudo-work because they appear to be work related. Indeed, it is difficult to make such a distinction on casual inspection. If we take a closer look, however, certain revealing clues become apparent. First of all, how long is the person taking over the activity? If it is work related, then it should not take long and the person is not likely to be too precise in how exact the tidying is, for example. However, if it is avoidance pseudo-work, the person takes an inordinately long time over the activity, which he or she carries out with almost obsessive precision. Secondly, how frequently does the person perform the activity? If it is work related, then the person carries out the activity once, while if it is pseudo-work the person repeats the activity fairly frequently instead of getting down to the real work. Thirdly, does the completion of the activity lead to real work being done? If it is work related the person gets down to the real business of studying as soon as the activity has been completed. If it is basically avoidance in nature, however, the completion of the task does not lead to the initiation of the real business of studying. Rather, the student thinks enough has been done for the day and decides to 'finish work', which is a rationalization. Finally, in his or her heart of hearts, can the person admit to the avoidance nature of these pseudo-work activities? You will note from the above discussion that a person can easily deceive him- or herself that he or she is engaged in real work when in fact what is engaged in is pseudo-work, discomfort-avoidance procrastination. If, however, the student can be honest about it, the person often knows deep down whether he or she is actually working or engaged in pseudo-work avoidance.

It follows from all this that part of adopting an anti-procrastination philosophy involves admitting to oneself that one is avoiding discomfort, seeing the long-term futility of doing so and then courting and staying with discomfort until one becomes comfortable doing the task that is worth tackling in the long run.

PURPOSIVE BEHAVIOUR IV: TO REDUCE THE INTENSITY OF AN EMOTIONAL STATE

If a person cannot stop an emotional state or take steps to avoid experiencing it, there is still the opportunity of reducing its intensity. This applies to both negative and positive emotional states. Let me consider this principle by dealing first with how people tend to minimize negative emotional states.

Georgina is a 45-year-old woman who experiences anxiety and occasional panic attacks while shopping. Prior to seeking professional help for these problems she developed a number of behavioural strategies, the purpose of which was to reduce or minimize her anxiety as best she could. Thus she developed a number of distraction techniques to use when she became anxious.

First, she would sing nursery rhymes in her head. This is a form of covert behaviour which she used to distract herself from her anxiety and which worked temporarily by reducing her anxiety level.

Whenever this method proved unsuccessful, she would read her shopping list, *sotto voce*. This is a form of verbal behaviour which again had the intent and effect of bringing her anxiety within manageable limits, albeit temporarily.

When her anxiety began to spiral into panic, she used more overt forms of behaviour to bring her feelings under some sort of control. If she was shopping with her husband or with a friend, she would grip tightly the other person's arm so that she did not faint – dizziness and the inference that one will faint is a common symptom of intense anxiety or panic. When her panic grew in intensity, Georgina would grip her shopping trolley so hard that her knuckles would turn white. At the peak of her panic, when she thought that she was beginning to have a heart attack – again a not uncommon inference in panic states – Georgina would stop walking and rest against a supporting wall until her feelings of panic reduced in intensity and became barely manageable anxiety.

At this point, Georgina would get the person accompanying her to queue up to pay for the shopping while she left the supermarket, an overt behavioural strategy which was designed to eliminate her negative feelings and which invariably had the effect. On the rare occasion when she went shopping on her own, Georgina would abandon her shopping trolley in an aisle and run out of the supermarket, which again served to rid her of her panicky feelings.

The above pattern of covert, verbal and overt behaviours, all designed to reduce the intensity of anxious and panicky feelings, is typical of those who suffer from panic attacks.

We can also use a number of behavioural strategies to reduce the intensity of positive emotional states although, as you can appreciate, we employ these less frequently than we use strategies to reduce the intensity of negative states. Why would we want to reduce the intensity of positive emotional states? We may do so because we believe that we do not deserve to be so happy or to experience so much pleasure. We may think this either because we consider that we have not done anything to merit such happiness or pleasure or because it is not right for us to be so happy when others whom we know are unhappy. These two views are frequently expressions of an irrational belief: I must not retain advantages when I have not done anything to deserve them or when others whom I care about are disadvantaged.

A second reason why we may act to reduce the intensity of positive emotional states is because we fear that something very bad may happen if we are that happy. I call this the 'evil eye' belief. Here we believe that we must not feel so good because if we do we will be penalized or even punished for our good fortune. This is particularly the case when we consider that we have not done anything to merit such happiness or pleasure. If we do we are tempting fate and we must act to reduce the intensity of our happiness before the evil eye, or some deity or spirit, spies our good fortune and brings misfortune on our heads to 'even up the score'.

We may also act to reduce the intensity of our positive feelings because we fear that we may lose control if we do not. Here our irrational belief is likely to be: 'I must not lose control and if I do terrible things may happen.'

This belief and the pleasure-reducing activities that leads to them often occur in the area of sex, particularly orgasm. For example, Fiona, a 27-year-old woman, sought counselling for anorgasmia (failure to achieve orgasm during intercourse). It transpired that she felt 'unable to let go' during intercourse with her husband. Whenever she began to feel a certain degree of pleasure she would distract herself either by thinking neutral thoughts or by changing her physical position to reduce the intensity of her positive feelings. Fiona was helped through counselling to overcome this problem by first learning to experience orgasm through masturbation (which she had never practised). She learned here that she could experience orgasm without losing total control of herself and then was able to transfer this insight to lovemaking with her husband.

PURPOSIVE BEHAVIOUR V: TO INTENSIFY AN EMOTIONAL
STATE

People have been taking steps to intensify their positive emotional states since time immemorial. The desire to experience more pleasure and to feel happier has motivated people to experiment with unusual and, in some cases, highly dangerous behavioural practices. When due care and attention is taken during attempts to intensify positive emotional states and there are no long-term negative effects of such behaviour, then there is usually no problem. Indeed, some highly erotic, safe sexual practices have emerged from people's quest to increase their pleasure.

Quite frequently, however, and especially when a person holds an irrational belief about intensification of pleasure, for example: 'I must increase the low or moderate level of pleasure that I feel and damn the consequences', he or she is likely to engage in behaviour that is more dangerous and self-defeating. The following is a tragic example of the dangers of seeking to intensify one's positive emotional state in a demanding, musturbatory manner.

Recently, in Britain, an MP was found dead in his flat. It was believed that he died from asphyxiation as a result of engaging in a sexual practice known as auto-erotic asphyxia. This term describes the practice, mainly engaged in by men, whereby a person strives to intensify his experience of orgasm by cutting off temporarily the supply of oxygen to his brain. This is accomplished by such methods as tying a ligature tightly around one's neck or placing a plastic bag over one's head. As you can tell from my description, this is a highly dangerous practice which, in Britain, accounts for around 200 deaths a year.

So far I have referred to ways in which people may intensify their physical pleasure without recourse to mood-altering drugs. Now I briefly discuss the many ways in which we use artificial means to amplify our pleasure. People have been using substances to intensify their positive experiences throughout history. These substances vary from the slightly unhealthy to the highly toxic and addictive. It is important here to distinguish between what effect the person expects the substance to induce and the substance's actual effect. Thus, someone may take LSD wishing to intensify his or her positive mood, but the actual effect may be very different – he or she may have a 'bad trip'. From the present analysis it is the person's expectations which guide his or her behaviour.

It is not only in the realm of physical pleasure that we strive to intensify our positive emotional states. We also act to intensify our sense of meaning and purpose. Thus, we may develop a growing interest in a project and choose to deepen that interest, and the sense of personal meaning that accompanies it, through behaviours which increase our active involvement in that project. These may include information-seeking activities, actively involving ourselves with others who share our interests, and carrying out new mini-projects to add to our own, and other people's, knowledge and interest.

Less frequently, people may act to intensify a negative emotional state. This happens particularly with guilt. Let me give an example. Bernice, a 37-year-old woman, has successfully kept to a weight-reducing diet for a week. Then, at a social gathering she eats more than her diet allows. She feels guilty about this because she believes that she is 'a greedy pig who absolutely shouldn't have let myself go like that'. When she arrives home, still feeling very guilty, she opens the door of the refrigerator and embarks on a huge eating 'binge'. Predictably she intensifies her guilt. It is important to note that Bernice's 'binging' behaviour could have had several different purposes. For example, she may have embarked on a binge to terminate her feelings of guilt, however temporarily. Yet, she considered it an example of guilt-intensifying behaviour. This is what she said later:

> When I got home from the party, I really felt bad, really guilty. I'd done so well on the diet and then in a matter of hours I felt that I had blown it. I remember thinking when I got home, 'Right now I'm going to do something to really feel guilty about.' So I went on an enormous binge. That did the trick!

PURPOSE BEHAVIOUR VI: TO MAINTAIN AN EMOTIONAL STATE

After a morning swim at the local swimming pool, I like to have a long hot shower. I notice that I have developed a number of washing rituals, the purpose of which, I have discovered, is to lengthen the time I spend in the shower. Why do I spend so long in the shower? It is not to ensure that I am perfectly clean! Rather it is to maintain, for as long as possible, the pleasurable feelings I get from being under the hot, steamy water.

The points that I made with respect to behaviour which is designed to initiate or intensify positive emotional states, are also relevant to behaviour, the purpose of which is to maintain such a state. Such behaviour is problematic (1) if it stems from an irrational belief – in which case the person is likely to maintain the positive state for longer than is healthy for him; (2) if it is intrinsically unhealthy for the individual, e.g. if it involves the use of drugs; and (3) if it interferes with the person's healthy goals. Otherwise, there is probably nothing wrong with behaviour, the purpose of which is to maintain our positive feelings.

An example of behaviour whose purpose is to maintain a negative emotional state is procrastination, which is designed to keep the person in a chronic negative state known as a rut, and which also serves to stop the person from experiencing more acute negative feelings. The person puts off doing anything which might result in getting out of the rut because from this perspective it appears that there are only two choices: either he or she feels anxious if he or she moves out of this rut (because the person holds an irrational belief about change); or he or she feels a comfortable, but negative, sense of lack of fulfilment. Faced with such a choice, it is understandable why someone would act to stay in a negative rut.

Of course the person does have other options. For example, it is possible to do something to identify, challenge and change the irrational beliefs that underpin this acute fear of change. In the absence of other perceived options, however, the person will often act to remain in this rut. Thus, when faced with the prospect of gaining promotion, the person might find him- or herself forgetting to hand in the application on time, or not doing well at the promotion interview. As I have mentioned before, such behaviour is not deliberate in the sense that the person says consciously to himself, 'Quick, I need to find some way of remaining in my rut. I know, I will forget to hand my application form in.' Nevertheless, the person acts as if this is what he believes.

PURPOSIVE BEHAVIOUR VII: TO ELICIT A RESPONSE FROM
THE PHYSICAL ENVIRONMENT

Imagine that you have a bank card which you can use in a wall cash dispenser machine. You insert the card into the appropriate aperture and follow a number of simple instructions which are flashed up on the machine's screen. Why do you do this? Simply because you want cash and you have learned that if you follow a number of steps you will receive the amount you requested. This is an everyday example of behaviour the purpose of which is to elicit an immediate response from the physical environment. If you fail to receive your cash on a number of occasions when you insert your card you will at some point refrain from carrying out this behavioural sequence.

Similar principles operate when behaviour is designed to elicit a long-term response from the physical environment. If you are a farmer, you are prepared to put in a great deal of effort to plant seeds on the assumption that this effort will yield a crop much later in the year. If this outcome does not occur in response to a small number of planting attempts, you will be loath to continue your planting behaviour unless you can identify what has gone wrong and can take remedial steps.

Thus, if your behaviour is designed to elicit an immediate or long-term response from the physical environment, you are likely to continue your behaviour if it produces that response and to discontinue your behaviour if it does not produce the response. At what point you will decide to discontinue depends on a number of complex factors which will vary from situation to situation. One important variable concerns a person's beliefs. If a person holds an irrational belief, he or she is more likely to persist with unsuccessful goal-directed behaviour than if that person thinks rationally. The reasons for this persistence are twofold. First, if the person believes that he or she must get what they want from the physical environment, then the person is more likely to keep striving for the goal when it is objectively clear that it cannot be achieved than if he or she holds a comparable rational belief: 'I want to get what I want, but I don't have to get it.' The rigid demand will interfere with the ability to see clearly that the goal is not achievable, while flexible preference will aid objectivity. Secondly, this person's rigid insistence that what he or she wants must be obtained from the physical environment will interfere with the ability to identify and experiment with alternative behaviours, one of which may help to achieve the goal. By contrast, the person's flexible preference will encourage him or her to stand back and consider other behavioural options.

If your behaviour is sometimes rewarded with the intended response and sometimes not, you will continue this behaviour far longer than if your behaviour consistently goes unrewarded. This principle of intermittent reinforcement of behaviour leading to the persistence of that behaviour is the rule that accounts for the maintenance of gambling, for example, Again, you will be more likely to persist with intermittently reinforced behaviour if you think irrationally about your goal than if you think rationally about it.

PURPOSIVE BEHAVIOUR VIII: TO ELICIT A RESPONSE FROM THE INTERPERSONAL ENVIRONMENT

We frequently act to elicit a response from other people. Again, as mentioned earlier, it is important to distinguish between a behaviour's purpose and its effect, because in the interpersonal arena we may well elicit the opposite response to that which we intend. Let me give an example of such behaviour.

1 To punish the other person
2 To get what I want
3 To get the other person to make the first move
4 To extract proof of caring from the other person

Figure 4.1 *Interpersonal purposes of sulking*

Interpersonal Purposes of Sulking

A number of years ago I published the first ever book written on sulking, *The Incredible Sulk* (Dryden, 1992). Before I wrote that book, I (together with my research assistant, Caroline Dearden) interviewed a number of women on their experiences of sulking – we could not find any men who would admit to sulking! As part of that research, I looked at the purposive aspects of sulking. In considering the types of interpersonal responses that people who sulk hope to elicit from others (see Figure 4.1), I will use the actual words of the women we interviewed to illustrate my points. Bear in mind when considering these interpersonal purposes that sulking itself stems from a set of irrational beliefs about certain activating events at A. If the person thought more rationally about these events he or she would not sulk. Rather they would assert themselves constructively with the other person concerned – behaviour which would seek a different, healthier set of responses from the other. See *The Incredible Sulk* for a fuller discussion of this issue.

To Punish the Other Person

Here the person wants to elicit a 'feeling' response in another, but in a way that avoids head-on confrontation. As Rosita noted, 'Sulking is a weapon to show that I have been upset and to retaliate without an actual confrontation . . . to make that person feel bad.'

To Get What I Want

Here the person finds that sulking works because it achieves what he or she wants. Jackie offers her opinion that 'because men in general are pretty insensitive, usually in order to make your point you have to impinge upon their lives and make them uncomfortable'. Jackie has discovered that sulking works for her because it impinges on her husband and makes him uncomfortable. As Jackie says, 'I regard sulking as a means to an end . . . to get what I want. . . . Sulking really can be quite a powerful weapon . . . I am not giving it up.'

Getting the Other Person to Make the First Move

As I said in *The Incredible Sulk*:

> Getting the other to make the first move is frequently based on the unconstructive idea:
>
> 'I must be treated fairly and since you have treated me unfairly, it's awful. Poor me!' The resulting feeling of hurt then leads to the attitude 'You must make the first move to make me feel better.' In order for this purpose to work, we have to remain in reasonable proximity with the other to be available to receive his or her first move. (Dryden, 1992: 39)

Mary illustrates this purpose quite well: 'If I sulk it's because I'm hurt and I want someone to come to me. I want the attention brought to me. I want someone to come to me and say "I'm sorry, I didn't mean it." I want them to come to me and apologise to me, so it's manipulative.'

To Extract Proof of Caring from the Other Person

This purpose differs from the one described above because, in the previous example the person sulks to get an apology from the other person, whereas here the person sulks to elicit caring from the other. Sometimes the other person is made to work quite hard in this respect. As Pamela says, 'When I sulk, I really make it difficult for John to find out what's wrong. If he persists long enough, and sometimes it's a very long time, I know that he loves me and then I'll tell him what's wrong.'

As these examples show once again, a single piece of behaviour can have quite different interpersonal purposes. It follows then that if you want to identify the interpersonal purpose of behaviour such as sulking it is important to do so from the perspective of the person responsible for the behaviour. It would be easy, for example, to view sulking simply as a manipulative ploy to get the person what he or she wants. However, as the examples in this section show, this is not the case.

PURPOSIVE BEHAVIOUR IX: TO ACT IN A WAY THAT IS
CONSISTENT WITH ONE'S VALUES, STANDARDS AND LONG-
TERM GOALS

I was once told an interesting story to demonstrate that people can act in accordance with their own behavioural standards and not just in response to the behaviour of others. Two businessmen travelled to work every day by train. When they reached their destination, one of the men was in the habit of buying a daily newspaper from a nearby newspaper vendor. Every day the vendor growled at the man and every day the man was very polite in response. This happened every working day for two years before the other man enquired of his colleague: 'Why are you so polite to the newspaper vendor when he is so rude to you?' The other man replied: 'Because I choose to act according to my standard of politeness rather than according to his standard of rudeness.'

This example nicely demonstrates the point that I wish to make here: that a person's behaviour can have the purpose of actualizing his or her values, standards and long-term goals. To do this, the person does have to think rationally. Thus, the man in the above example probably holds the following rational belief: 'I don't have to respond to the newspaper vendor in the manner in which he treats me.'

A friend of mine once worked in an organization where pilfering of office supplies was rife. My friend, however, not only refused to take even a single paper clip, he reported the pilfering of his work colleagues to the head of the organization, who instituted an enquiry into the whole affair. My friend did this even though he guessed that he would be shunned by his colleagues as a result. This was, in fact, what happened and my friend spent a very uncomfortable six months in a hostile work environment before he left the company for another job. My friend admitted that it would have been very easy for him to keep quiet about the pilfering, but he said that doing so would have gone against his moral values of honesty and good citizenship. He chose to act in a way that was consistent with his values, even though doing so led to a great deal of personal discomfort. He was able to do this because he had a rational belief about receiving disapproval from others and about being uncomfortable.

Finally, let me consider that behaviour which is used to help the individual pursue his or her long-term goals. REBT considers that it is a mark of positive mental health for a person to pursue long-term goals while tolerating the short-term discomfort of doing so.

About a year ago, I decided to embark on an exercise regimen whereby I would jog or swim 20 minutes a day, five days a week. I decided on this programme in order to maintain my health. Every day, when I wake up, I do not want to go out to exercise and yet I go. I do so first because I choose to behave in a way that is consistent with my long-term health goals and is inconsistent with my short-term comfort goals, and secondly, because I have a rational belief about short-term discomfort.

In the following two sections of this chapter, I discuss two concepts that are important in understanding REBT's view of behaviour: action tendencies and response options. In doing so, I concentrate on situations where the person is experiencing an unhealthy negative emotion.

Action Tendencies

Whenever a person experiences an emotion, he has a tendency to act in a broad manner. As we saw in Chapter 1, different emotions lead to different action tendencies. In the previous section, I made the point that much behaviour is purposive and certainly when we tend to act in certain ways depending on the emotion we are experiencing, our resulting behaviour is purposive. Under these circumstances our specific behaviour serves to help us achieve a particular goal. However, these goals or purposes which shape our behaviour are influenced to a large extent by the emotions we experience. Thus action tendencies are in large part determined by emotions.

When a person experiences unhealthy negative emotions, the goals are likely to be self-protective in the short term – they influence the person to act in ways that reduce or terminate these emotions – but self-defeating in the longer term – they do not help the person to face up to and deal constructively with negative As. When that person experiences healthy negative emotions, however, his or her goals are more likely to be self-enhancing in both the short and the long term, because that person will be less likely to strive to reduce or terminate these emotions and will be more likely to deal constructively with the negative events at A.

Action tendencies are general categories of behaviour rather than specific pieces of behaviour. Moreover, different specific behaviours can actualize a given action tendency. For example, a major action tendency that flows from the emotion of anger urges us to attack the person about whom we are angry. There are a number of ways in which we can carry out such an attack: directly, either physically or verbally; or indirectly, such as by attacking the person's reputation by spreading rumours behind his or her back, or by destroying a valued possession without him or her knowing who perpetrated such an attack. Each of these different specific behaviours is a concrete expression of the same, much broader action tendency.

Response Options

Response options are behavioural possibilities that exist in a given situation. Such options might include ways of acting which serve

- to actualize the action tendency;
- to go against the action tendency in a way that is constructive; and
- to compensate the person influenced by the action tendency.

Additionally, one can choose ways of acting that are not related to the action tendency.

Furthermore, response options that actualize some of the other purposes of behaviour listed on p. 51 and discussed earlier in this chapter are also relevant in this context. Let me illustrate two of the types of response option listed above by continuing with the example of anger and the associated action tendency of attack. I have already shown that we can attack another person with whom we are angry by choosing from a number of specific attack-related response options, so let me begin by discussing constructive response options that go against this action tendency.

CONSTRUCTIVE RESPONSE OPTIONS THAT GO AGAINST AN ACTION TENDENCY

A constructive alternative to attacking another person is to assert ourselves with him or her. In order to do this effectively, we need to hold rational rather than irrational beliefs. While it is possible for us to assert ourselves constructively with another person when we are angry, such assertive behaviour is likely to break down if that other person does not respond in a similarly constructive manner.

Thus, if we are to utilize a constructive response option that goes against an action tendency that is based on an unhealthy negative emotion (in this case anger), we first need to challenge and change the irrational beliefs that underpin such an emotion. If we do this, we will experience a healthy negative emotion (in this case annoyance) and will be influenced by a different action tendency that stems from this emotion (in this case, to deal effectively with the A that we were previously angry about). If we do this, we are likely to sustain assertive behaviour because this response option is now consistent with our new action tendency.

RESPONSE OPTIONS THAT COMPENSATE THE PERSON INFLUENCED BY AN ACTION TENDENCY

When we choose a response option that allows us to compensate for an unhealthy negative emotion such as anger, we are still influenced by this emotion, but are able to refrain from actualizing the attack action tendency. For example, when we are angry at another person, we may choose to be exceptionally nice to that person. In this case, our nice behaviour enables us to compensate for our anger.

Such compensatory behaviour serves a number of purposes. First, it may help us to avoid experiencing unacceptable emotions. Thus, many people believe that it is wrong to be angry and that they must not experience such an emotion. Being nice to the person with whom we feel an underlying anger allows us to remain unaware that we are experiencing this forbidden feeling. Secondly, it may protect us from getting into unwanted trouble with the person with whom we are angry. If we are angry with someone who has power and influence over us then it might not be wise for us to express our anger to that person. So, because we are angry, we compensate by being extra nice to the other person. The same principle applies when we believe that we need the approval of the person with whom we are angry. If we were to attack the person, we would be scared that he or she would disapprove of us, so, again, we compensate for our anger by being overly nice to that person.

The reason why we act especially nicely to the other person under these conditions is that we think that our anger would show if we were to act in an everyday manner. Our extra-nice behaviour serves to disguise our anger from the other person so that (1) he or she cannot use any power against us; or (2) he or she does not disapprove of us. If we were annoyed rather than angry, we would be less likely to resort to the use of this compensatory mechanism because we would be more in control of our feelings and we would be more likely to assert ourselves in a way that does not alienate the other person.

Behavioural Competence

REBT recognizes that people may or may not have certain responses in their behavioural repertoire, and it also acknowledges that when these behaviours are in their repertoire, they perform them at varying levels of skill. If a person does not possess such a skill in his or her behavioural repertoire, REBT notes that this situation may have arisen as a result of that person holding irrational beliefs. Thus, if you believe that you must do well in conversing with members of the opposite sex, you may avoid speaking to them; because you avoid doing so, you deprive yourself of valuable opportunities for developing your social skills in this area of your life.

However, it is important for REBT therapists to avoid taking an inflexible line and assuming that skill deficits always stem from irrational beliefs. They may do, but there are a number of other factors that explain why a person has not developed certain behavioural skills. These include lack of opportunity, exposure to poor role models, lack of aptitude and lack of positive reinforcement for skilled performance. A person may develop irrational beliefs as a result of failing to acquire certain skills and, as I have just described, failure to develop skills may stem from the person holding irrational beliefs. The situation here is 'both/and' rather than 'either/or'. This both/and explanation is also relevant when we account for variations in skill level among people.

REBT therapists also consider the inferences and evaluative beliefs that people construct about their level of behavioural competence. For example, at the inferential level, people can either underestimate or overestimate their level of skill or give an improvement in skill level a particular inferential meaning (e.g. 'Now that I can converse more skilfully with women, I will soon lose my virginity'). At the level of evaluative beliefs, people may rate themselves for having a certain level of skill (e.g. 'I'm not as socially skilled as I absolutely should be and as a result I'm no good' – irrational belief) or may evaluate the effort that it may take to become more skilful (e.g. 'It will take a lot of practice to learn more productive study skills. I wish it were easier, but it doesn't have to be any easier than it is. I can tolerate the effort involved' – rational belief).

In the following chapter, I will further consider the issue of behaviour as it interacts with A, B, and emotional Cs.

Reference

Dryden, W. (1992) *The Incredible Sulk*. London: Sheldon.

5
Complex Relationships among the ABCs of REBT

In Chapter 1, I gave a brief overview of the ABCs of rational emotive behaviour therapy. In this chapter, I will be more specific in detailing some of the complex relationships and interactions that can exist among the ABCs.[1] To make a complex situation even more complicated we also have to consider a person's goals or purposes, which Albert Ellis (1991) calls Gs. I begin by considering goals and how they influence and are influenced by the ABCs of REBT. I call this process of mutual influence 'reciprocal influence', and I consider various types of reciprocal influence throughout this chapter.

Reciprocal Influence I: How Goals (Gs) Influence and Are Influenced by the ABCs of REBT

People bring their goals and purposes (Gs) to the ABCs of their experience and these goals have an influence on the ABCs. In turn, their goals can be influenced by these ABCs. Thus, if a person has the goal of achieving promotion at work, this goal will affect and be affected by his or her ABCs in the following illustrative ways.

Gs AND ACTUAL As

The person's goal (G) of achieving promotion at work will influence the actual events (As) that he or she chooses to create and encounter. Thus, a man may choose to stay late at work (i.e. he creates and encounters more work-oriented As); he may refuse to go to the pub after work with his friends (i.e. he creates and encounters fewer socially oriented As); and he may run into conflict with his wife who complains to him that she and her children are being deprived of his company (i.e. he creates and encounters more stressful family-related As). The more important his goal of achieving promotion is to him, the more likely it is that he will create and encounter these actual As.

This chapter was originally published in W. Dryden, *Invitation to Rational-Emotive Psychology*. London: Whurr, 1994.

In addition, this man's goals are influenced by actual As. For example, if he consistently is rejected for promotion at work, eventually he may well relinquish this goal. Whether he thinks rationally or irrationally about these rejections will, of course, have a mediating effect on whether he persists with or relinquishes his goal. However, independent of his beliefs, the more actual rejections he gets, the more likely it is that he will relinquish his goal.

Gs AND INFERRED As

The man's goal of achieving promotion at work (G) will also influence the types of inference that he makes about actual events. For example, if his manager praises him for a piece of work that he has done (actual A), he may make the inference 'This means that he will put in a good word for me with the boss.' Whereas, if his manager criticizes him for the piece of work, he may infer 'My manager won't support my application for promotion.' The more important his goal of achieving promotion is to him, the more likely it will be that he will make these inferences and the more he will consider these inferences to be facts.

In turn, a person's goal will be influenced by the types of inference that he or she makes. For example, the more positive the inferences, the more important the goal is likely to become. Conversely, the more negative the inferences, the more likely it is that he or she will relinquish or change the goals (e.g. by setting his or her sights lower). Again this process will be influenced by the types of belief held about these inferences, but independent of what he or she believes, the relationship as stated between the impact of inferences on the person's goals tends to exist.

Gs AND Bs

When a man, for example, has the goal of achieving promotion at work, this goal influences the types of belief that the person has about whether or not he achieves this goal. If he does achieve it, he may believe rationally: 'It is good that I have been promoted, but it doesn't make me a better person', or irrationally: 'It is wonderful that I have been promoted. What a great person I am.' However, if he fails to realize his goal, he may rationally believe: 'It is unfortunate that I haven't been promoted. I am still a fallible human being though', or irrationally conclude: 'It is terrible that I failed to get my promotion. What a worthless person I am.'

The more important the person's goal of obtaining promotion is to him, the stronger his rational beliefs will be (if he thinks rationally about his goal) and the more rigid will be his irrational beliefs (if he thinks irrationally about his goal).

In general, a person's goals (Gs) do not lead the person to have beliefs of indifference, e.g. 'It doesn't matter if I am promoted or not.' If the person does have such a belief, it is usually a defence against the unhealthy negative emotions that stem from his irrational beliefs, rather than as a direct result of his goals.

Goals are, in turn, affected by the types of belief the person holds about his job promotion. Thus, if a person holds irrational beliefs about the promotion, he is more likely to relinquish or modify this goal than if he holds a set of rational beliefs about it. This is true especially if he encounters (or creates) negative actual As or makes negative inferences.

THE IMPACT OF Gs ON EMOTIONAL Cs

When a person has the goal of achieving a job promotion, as in the above example, then this will have an impact on his emotions at C, although usually this will occur as a result of the interaction between his goals and the types of belief that he holds about the promotion. Thus, if he thinks rationally about the sought-after promotion (G), he will experience healthy positive feelings about the promotion if he obtains it (or if it looks as if he will obtain it) – e.g. pleasure, joy or eagerness, or he will experience healthy negative feelings if he does not obtain it (or if it looks as if he will not obtain it) – e.g. disappointment, sadness and concern. The intensity of these healthy feelings will depend on the degree of importance of the person's goal and the strength of conviction he has in his rational beliefs. For example, the person will experience strong feelings of sadness when he fails to achieve his promotion if this goal is important to him and if his conviction in his rational belief is strong.

However, if he thinks irrationally about the sought-after promotion (G), he will experience unhealthy positive feelings about the promotion if he obtains it (or if it looks as if he will obtain it) – e.g. mania, or he will experience unhealthy negative feelings if he does not obtain it (or if it looks as if he will not obtain it) – e.g. hurt, depression and anxiety.

Again, the intensity of these unhealthy feelings will depend on the degree of importance of the person's goal and the degree of rigidity with which he holds irrational beliefs. For example, the person will experience strong feelings of depression when he fails to achieve his promotion if this goal is important to him and if he rigidly adheres to his irrational belief.

Turning to the influence of a person's emotions on his goals, it is probably the case that when the person is feeling positive he will maintain or even increase the sense of importance that he gives to his goal of achieving promotion at work. If he is feeling manic (which is a positive unhealthy emotion), he will tend to consider his goal all-important, while if he is feeling very pleased (which is a positive healthy emotion) he will tend to consider his goal to be important, but not all-important. Similarly, if he experiences an unhealthy negative emotion he will think of his goal as either all-important (when feeling anxious) or unimportant (when feeling depressed). Whereas if he experiences a healthy negative emotion, e.g. concern or sadness, he will still consider his goal to be important, but not crucial.

Gs AND BEHAVIOURAL Cs

When the person has the goal of achieving a job promotion, this has a decided impact on his or her behaviour. The following behaviours are illustrative of this impact and need to be compared with the situation where the person does not have this goal. There will be a tendency to:

- work harder;
- seek allies who can help him or her to achieve the goal;
- take more care over work;
- be more punctual about arriving at work on time;
- volunteer for extra work;
- stay at work later than his or her scheduled leaving time;
- find ways of showing the boss how well and how hard he or she is doing.

There are other salient issues that it is important to take into account here. These include the importance of the person's goal and the nature of his or her beliefs about achieving that goal.

Thus, the more important the goal is to the person, the more likely it is that he or she will act in the ways illustrated above, and the more effort will be invested in these activities. In addition, the constructive implementation of these activities is dependent to a large (but not exclusive) degree on the types of belief that the person holds about achieving the goal. Thus if a rational belief is held about achieving the goal (e.g. 'I would like to be promoted at work, but there is no reason why I must achieve my goal'), then REBT would hypothesize that the person will be more subtle and more successful at implementing the behavioural strategies listed above than if an irrational belief is held about goal achievement (e.g. 'I absolutely have to obtain my promotion'). As noted in Chapter 1, rational beliefs tend to promote constructive, goal-seeking behaviour, while irrational beliefs tend to impede such behaviour.

Alternatively, a person's behaviour can influence his or her goals. Thus, if the person works hard at the job, this will tend to reinforce the importance of the goal of achieving promotion, whereas if he or she procrastinates or shirks at the duties, such behaviour will tend to weaken the importance of the goal.

Reciprocal Influence II: How Actual As Influence and Are Influenced by Inferred As and Bs

Actual activating events (actual As) are events that occur in reality. They are distinguished from inferred events in that they do not contain any of the person's inferences which add meaning to the event. Actual events interact with a person's inferences, beliefs, emotions, behaviours and goals in complex ways. I will give some examples below to illustrate this complexity.

ACTUAL As AND INFERRED As

The relationship between actual and inferred As is often influenced by the person's goals. Thus, when a person has a goal such as a job promotion then he or she is likely to infer that certain actual As will help to achieve the goals, while other actual As will impede the quest to achieve his or her goal. The more important is the goal, the more likely it is that the person will make such inferences.

The more negative an event is, the more likely it is that the person will make negative inferences about that event and the more distorted these negative inferences are likely to be.[2] This explains why people are often faced with a double dose of negativity at A – one related to the actual event and the other related to his or her inferences.

Let me take rape as an example. Being raped is obviously a very negative activating event for the vast majority of people. As such, it will strongly influence those who have been raped to make highly distorted negative inferences such as 'I'll never get over the experience', 'I'm much more likely to be raped again' and 'It was my fault.' In saying this, I am neither condoning the crime of rape nor blaming the victim for making such inferences. All I am doing is pointing out that when people face very negative actual events, it is highly likely that they will make distorted negative inferences about these actual As.

The types of inference a person makes can influence the actual As to which a person pays attention. For example, if a person infers that there is a good chance that he or she will be promoted at work, then he or she is more likely to pay attention to actual As that are consistent with such an inference (e.g. instances of people complimenting his or her work) than to actual As that are inconsistent with this inference (e.g. when the person's work is ignored or criticized). This pattern is reversed when the person infers that there is a poor chance that he or she will gain promotion. This effect is accentuated if the person holds an irrational belief about promotion, and attenuated if he or she holds a rational belief.

ACTUAL As AND Bs

Actual As can influence the types of belief a person holds, and a similar point can be made with respect to the impact of actual As on beliefs to that made above about the impact of actual As on inferred As. Namely, the more negative the actual A, the more likely it is that the person will think irrationally about it. Thus, if a person encounters a mildly negative or moderately negative actual A, then he or she may hold a version of the following rational belief: 'I would prefer it if this event had not occurred, but there's no reason why it absolutely should not have happened.' However, if the person encounters a highly negative actual A, then it is more likely that he or she will hold a version of the following irrational belief than if faced with a less negative actual A: 'Because I really don't want this event to occur, therefore it absolutely should not happen.'

When highly negative events do happen to people, these As often trigger interesting irrationalities in these people which would be triggered less frequently by less aversive actual As. Some people irrationally believe, for example, that when they experience an adversity: 'It must only be a small one', or 'It absolutely should not have been as bad as it is.' Such people believe that they absolutely should be immune to such highly aversive actual As. This is often what underlies the statement: 'I didn't think that this would ever happen to me.'

Other people believe in a kind of universal 'deservingness', where bad things happen only to those who deserve it. For example, when a mother loses her baby in a cot death, she may well believe irrationally (but understandably): 'Because neither my young baby nor anybody in my family has done anything to deserve this, it therefore absolutely should not have happened.'

When such tragic events happen to religious people, they either give up their faith, or their belief in God is severely tested because they believe, again irrationally, that: 'God absolutely should not have allowed such a tragedy to happen.' Rabbi Harold Kushner

(1982) has written an interesting book, entitled *When Bad Things Happen to Good People*, which deals with this issue more fully.

REBT keenly distinguishes between catastrophes and tragedies on the one hand, and the concept of 'awfulizing' on the other (see Chapter 1 for a fuller discussion of awfulizing). REBT acknowledges that such tragedies and catastrophes do happen in life and recognizes that it is very easy for most people to awfulize about them. Such awfulizing, according to Albert Ellis, is derived from a musturbatory belief, e.g. 'This tragedy absolutely should not have occurred and it is awful that it did.' Contrast this with the rational alternative: 'I would much prefer it if this tragedy did not exist, but unfortunately there is no reason why it absolutely should not have happened. It is tragic, but not the end of the world.' This latter belief reflects the REBT viewpoint that 'tragedies are not awful, but they are tragic'. I want to stress that this is not playing with words. Rather, this viewpoint represents a serious attempt to encourage people to be healthily distressed about tragedies without adding unhealthy emotional disturbance to adversity.

I also want to stress that the variable of time often interacts with highly aversive actual As and beliefs. While most people will think irrationally about the occurrence of actual tragedies in their lives when these events have just happened, the majority of these people will eventually think rationally about these actual As, although it may take some of them years to be able to do so.[3]

Some people unfortunately never stop thinking irrationally about such tragedies and live miserable lives as a result, while others are able to push such events out of their mind even though they still hold underlying irrational beliefs about the occurrences.[4]

A small minority of people are able to think rationally about tragedies even at the point of their occurrence. A well-known example is that of Gordon Wilson, whose daughter, Marie, was killed in the Enniskillen bombing that was carried out by the IRA, and in which Gordon Wilson, himself, was injured. Right after this tragedy, Wilson said that he felt no malice towards the bombers, which from an REBT perspective means that he held no anger-based irrationalities towards them. He claimed later that his belief in God enabled him to be malice-free. The question of the role of religious belief in encouraging such an immediate rational response to tragedy is one that merits scientific study.

A person's beliefs can also influence the actual events to which a person pays attention. I have already made this point when showing the impact of inferred As on actual As (see pp. 74–5). For example, if a person believes irrationally that he or she is worthless because of failure to gain promotion at work, then he or she will pay attention to actual instances of people pointing out his or her job deficiencies and fail to register actual instances of people pointing out the job strengths. However, if the person believes rationally that he or she is a fallible human being, even though he or she failed to obtain promotion, then that person will pay attention to both types of actual As.

Reciprocal Influence III: How Inferred As Influence and Are Influenced by Bs and Behavioural Cs

You will recall that inferences are hunches about reality which go beyond the data at hand and relate to matters of personal significance within the individual's personal domain. In this section, I will consider how inferences are reciprocally related to beliefs and behaviours.

INFERRED As AND Bs

When inferred As are negatively distorted they often (but not always) (1) stem from a person's irrational belief, and (2) trigger a further irrational belief. This can best be illustrated in the development of a panic attack where inferences and irrational beliefs interact at lightning speed to create mounting panic. This is illustrated in Figure 5.1.

Inferences that are less negatively distorted tend to trigger a person's irrational beliefs less frequently than inferences that are highly distorted negatively. Thus, when a person infers that not only will he or she fail to be promoted, but that he or she will also be made redundant, that person is more likely to think irrationally about this inferred A than about a prediction (i.e. predictive inference) that he or she will simply fail to be promoted.

A number of years ago I did an experiment with two colleagues that showed the impact of beliefs on inferences (Dryden et al., 1989). We asked one group of subjects to imagine that they held an irrational belief about spiders (i.e. 'I must not see a spider and it would be terrible if I did see one'), and a second group that they held a rational belief about spiders (i.e. 'I would prefer not to see a spider, but there is no reason why I must not see one. If I do see a spider, it would be bad, but not terrible'). Then we told them to imagine that they would be going into a room where a spider had been spotted and we asked them to answer a number of questions while holding to the belief that they were assigned. Here is a sample of the questions that we asked:

Actual A:	Feeling tense.
Inferred A:	I'm going to have trouble breathing.
Irrational belief:	I must be able to breathe more easily.
Inferred A:	I'm getting more anxious. I'm going to choke.
Irrational belief:	I must be able to control my breathing right now.
Inferred A:	I'm going to die.
Irrational belief:	I must not die in this fashion.
C:	Strong panic.

Figure 5.1   *Reciprocal influence between inferred As and irrational beliefs*

- How many spiders are there in the room?
- What is the size of the spider(s)?
- In which direction is (are) the spider(s) moving: towards you, away from you or in a random direction?

The results of this experiment showed that when subjects held an irrational belief about spiders, they estimated that there would be more spiders in the room, that the spiders would be larger and that the spiders were more likely to be moving towards them, than for those subjects who held a rational belief about spiders. This suggests that holding an irrational belief leads people to make more highly distorted negative inferences than holding a rational belief.

Interestingly enough, the differential effect of belief on inferences that were found in the spider experiment was accentuated when subjects were asked to imagine that they would be entering a dark room alone, and attenuated when they were asked to imagine that they would be entering a light room accompanied by a friend. This demonstrates the important role that actual As play in either exaggerating or minimizing the effect of beliefs on inferences.

INFERRED As AND BEHAVIOURAL Cs

When a person makes an inference about reality, he or she influences the way in which he or she tends to act (i.e. the action tendency) and the actual behaviour. This influence will be independent of his or her belief although, of course, beliefs will also play an important role here. Let me give an obvious example. Suppose you are walking alone at night down a dimly lit street and you hear a noise. Suppose you make the following inference; 'I am about to be mugged.' Whether you think rationally or irrationally about this you will have a tendency to take flight, to freeze or to turn and fight. Certainly, if you hold an irrational belief about your inference you will increase your chances of reacting in one of these three ways. But, even if you hold a rational belief about the prospect of being mugged, you will still tend to take flight, freeze or fight.

Conversely, if a person acts in a certain way, his behaviour will have an influence on the inferences he makes. For example, if a woman is at a party and approaches people, she is more likely to infer that these people are interested in talking to her than if she does not approach people.[5]

If the person does not approach people at the party, her lack of action on this occasion will prompt her to make inferences such as: 'They don't find me interesting. If they did, they would come up to talk to me', 'I don't have anything interesting to say to them, since if I did, I would go up to talk to them', and 'They all know each other. They look on me as an outsider.' Of course, she would be more likely to make such inferences if she held irrational beliefs as opposed to rational beliefs in this situation. However, if her beliefs are taken out of the picture, her action (of initiating conversation with others) is more likely to lead her to make positive inferences about others' reaction to her than her lack of action.

While taking action in this situation will in itself decrease the chances that the person will make negative inferences about others' reactions to her, such action provides her with direct feedback from others which, in most cases, contradicts any negative inferences that she might be making about the situation.[6]

However, if the person is inactive and does not initiate any conversation with others she does not get direct feedback from them to contradict her negative inferences. So, she is left with making inferences about why they have not approached her. In such a situation she is more likely to conclude that the reason they are not approaching her is because they do not find her interesting rather than the equally or more plausible inferential alternatives such as 'They are not approaching me because I am not approaching them,' or 'Maybe they think that I don't want to approach them, that's why they are not coming up to me'.

Reciprocal Influence IV: How Beliefs Influence and Are Influenced by Emotional and Behavioural Cs

I have already considered in this chapter the relationship between a person's beliefs and (a) the actual As she encounters, (b) the inferences she makes and (c) the goals she has. Here, I will look at the impact of emotional and behavioural Cs on the beliefs a person holds.

THE IMPACT OF EMOTIONS ON BELIEFS

While one of the principal tenets of REBT stresses the central role that beliefs play in determining a person's emotions, it is also the case that REBT recognizes that emotions can influence the beliefs that the person's holds. For example, if a person is depressed then he is more likely to think of himself as worthless than if he is sad, but not depressed. This is obviously the case when his original depression stems from ideas of worthlessness, but it is also likely to happen when his depression stems from other beliefs such as self-pity or other-pity ideas. This effect may well be mediated by beliefs, as when the person believes: 'I must not feel sorry for myself and I am worthless if I do.' However, this influence of emotions on beliefs may occur in a less direct way. It is well known that when a person is depressed, he will tend to think more about negative actual or inferred As than when he is sad, but not depressed. Thus, if the person is depressed about failing at something important, he will tend to retrieve more past failures (actual or inferred) from his memory than when he is sad. Having thus retrieved these failure experiences from his memory, the person can do one of two things: he can reinforce his already activated irrational belief, and he can use such evidence to create a new irrational belief.

In the first situation, the person focuses on the failure experiences that his depression has helped to retrieve from his memory and uses these as evidence to support his already activated irrational belief (i.e. 'I absolutely shouldn't have failed at this task and I am a failure for doing so. Not only that, but look at how many times I have failed in the past. This doubly proves what a failure I am').

Alternatively, in the second case, the retrieval of these past actual or inferred failures triggers a new irrational belief in the person. Having focused on some of his past failures, the person then creates the following irrationality: 'I now see that I have failed at quite a few things in my life. I absolutely should not have failed so much in life.'

Conversely, when the person is sad but not depressed about a present failure, he will tend to think of both past failures and past successes. When he does focus on past failures, he will be less likely to create an irrational belief about these failures when he is sad than when he is depressed.

THE IMPACT OF BEHAVIOURS ON BELIEFS

In Chapter 1 I showed how holding irrational beliefs influences the person to act in an unconstructive, self-defeating manner, while holding rational beliefs tends to promote more constructive, self-enhancing behaviour. As elsewhere, the relationship between beliefs and behaviour is reciprocal and behaviour can serve to reinforce existing beliefs or help trigger new ones.

For example, if a person holds an irrational belief that she is worthless and consequently withdraws from other people and sits for long periods alone in a darkened room, then she will be more likely to reinforce this belief than if she sought out company or engaged in an involving activity while alone. Similarly, if a person, while not depressed, sat alone in a darkened room, read only newspaper reports that detailed man's inhumanity to man and cut off contact with the outside world, then she is more likely to create irrational, depression-related beliefs than if she sat in a bright room, read newspaper reports dealing with good and bad news and responded to or initiated contact with other people.

Reciprocal Influence V: How Emotional Cs Influence and Are Influenced by Actual As and Inferred As

Earlier in this chapter, I considered how emotions are reciprocally related to a person's goals and beliefs. Here I look at the inter-relations between emotions, on the one hand, and actual As and inferred As, on the other.

EMOTIONS AND ACTUAL As

I have already noted that when a person encounters a highly aversive actual A, he is more likely to hold irrational beliefs than if he encounters a lesser actual adversity. It follows from this that the person is more likely to experience unhealthy negative emotions about highly negative actual As than about less negative ones.

Different unhealthy negative emotions are associated with different inferences. This, of course, is particularly the case when the person concerned holds irrational beliefs about the inference. However, a person's inferences (which you will recall are hunches about reality) may be an accurate reflection of an actual A. In this sense, different actual As, when they are actual embodiments of an inference pattern, are associated with different unhealthy negative emotions, again when the person thinks irrationally about the actual event.

Putting these two principles together – (a) that a person is more likely to experience an unhealthy negative emotion about a highly aversive actual A than about a less aversive actual event and (b) that when actual As embody inferences, then the person will experience different unhealthy negative emotions about different actual As when he thinks irrationally about them – we arrive at the following. A person will be more likely to experience different unhealthy negative emotions when he encounters actual As which embody different types of inferences when these actual As are highly aversive than when they are moderately or mildly aversive.

For example, when a person experiences an actual loss, he will be more likely to be depressed about it when the loss is a serious one than when it is less serious. Additionally, when a person encounters an actual threat, he is more likely to be anxious about it if the threat is great than if it is less great. Of course, these statements hold true when the person's beliefs are taken out of the picture. When we bring them back into the picture then they can either protect the person against unhealthy negative emotions or make it more likely that he will experience them. Thus, if a person holds a rational belief about a serious loss, he will be less likely to experience depression than if he holds an irrational belief about a less serious loss.

When we consider the effect of emotions on actual As, we need to bear in mind that behaviour often serves as a mediating variable here. When a person experiences an emotion she has a tendency to act in a certain way. If she then actualizes this tendency and behaves in a certain manner she may, through her behaviour, encounter certain actual As that she might not encounter if she did not act in that certain manner. Take, for example, a person who experiences anger towards a work colleague for threatening his self-esteem. When he is angry he has, you will recall from Chapter 1, a tendency to attack the source of this threat. Now, if he actualizes this tendency he may encounter one or more of the following actual As:

1 he may have a fight with his co-worker;
2 he may be disciplined for his unruly behaviour;
3 he may be fired for his aggression;
   and
4 he may get into trouble with the police as a result of the attack.

If he was annoyed but not angry about the inferred threat to his self-esteem, then he will have a different action tendency, which if actualized, will lead him to encounter a different set of actual As. Thus, his annoyance will lead him to assert himself with his co-worker in a constructive way which may well lead to better relations between them. Now, it is true that if the person is angry, he does not have to actualize his action tendency and attack the other person. However, he is more likely to attack his work colleague when he is angry than when he is annoyed and consequently his anger increases the chances that he will encounter one or more of the illustrative actual As listed above.

EMOTIONS AND INFERRED As

I discussed in Chapter 1, the influence that inferred As have on a person's emotions. Specifically, I showed that different inferences (or inferred As) are associated with different healthy negative emotions (when the person holds a set of rational beliefs about the inferred A) and with different unhealthy emotions (when the person holds a set of irrational beliefs about the inferred A).

Conversely, the way a person feels can influence the inferences that she makes about a given situation. Thus, if a person is already anxious, her anxiety will increase the likelihood that she will make threat-related inferences about the situation that she is in than if she is experiencing concern, but not anxiety. Also when she is in a situation that contains both threatening and non-threatening aspects, she is more likely to focus on the threatening features of the environment when she is already anxious than when she is already concerned.

As a further example if a person is already in a depressed state of mind he is more likely to make inferences about his past, present and future that relate to failure than he would if he is already experiencing sadness, but not depression.

Reciprocal Influence VI: How Behaviour Influences and is Influenced by As, Cs and Gs

I have already covered most of the interrelationships between behaviour and the other elements deemed important by REBT for a full understanding of how we function as humans. Thus, I have considered the ways in which behaviour has a reciprocal relationship with goals, with inferred As and with beliefs. I showed how behaviour based on emotion can influence the kind of actual As a person may encounter and the impact of actual As on emotion. I have alluded to the types of action tendencies a person may have in such situations. By extrapolating from action tendencies to behaviour, you can see how people may act in such circumstances.

This leaves the relationship between behaviour and emotion. In Chapter 1, I discussed fully the types of action tendency that are based on different healthy and unhealthy negative emotions. I have already shown the impact that emotions have on the ways in which a person tends to act. I will now discuss briefly the influence of behaviour on emotion.

THE IMPACT OF BEHAVIOUR ON EMOTION

The ways in which behaviour can influence emotion can best be seen in situations where a person already experiences an unhealthy negative emotion. Basically, when a person experiences such an emotion, the more he actualizes the action tendency on which that emotion is based, the more he will perpetuate that emotion in the longer term. However, the more he actualizes the action tendency associated with the relevant healthy negative alternative, the more chance he has of changing his unhealthy negative emotion to that healthy alternative.

Take anxiety, for example. If a person is anxious and withdraws from the situation (action tendency), then although he will experience an immediate reduction in anxiety, he increases the chances that he will become anxious in the same or similar situations in the future. This is because, by withdrawing, the person has strengthened the irrational beliefs that underpinned his anxiety in the first place. If the person is to deal with his anxiety productively, he needs to remain in the situation and tolerate his anxious feelings until he experiences healthy concern. In this case the person's behaviour has allowed him to remain in the situation where he can challenge and change his anxiety-based irrational beliefs, thus enabling him to experience the more healthy emotion of concern.

Notes

1. A full discussion of all possible interactions would merit a volume on its own. Consequently, I will discuss a sample of such interactions in this chapter.

2. This is generally the case if we assume that the person's beliefs are held constant. As we see later, a person's beliefs can augment or minimize the chances that he or she will make distorted negative inferences about actual As.

3. What happens in the intervening time period that enables people to think rationally about such tragic events is beyond the scope of this book.

4. Again a discussion of why some people can put such tragedies to the back of their mind while others cannot, even though both groups retain irrational beliefs about the events in question, is beyond the scope of this book.

5. This will not necessarily be the case if she holds an irrational belief such as 'I must entertain others and it is terrible if I do not', since she will think that others will find her boring if she does not entertain them sufficiently.

6. Again I want to stress that if the person holds an irrational belief in this situation such as 'I must be entertaining', then she will be more likely to distort such feedback in a negative direction (e.g. 'You see they did find me boring. They only laughed a little at my jokes').

References

Dryden, W., Ferguson, J. and McTeague, S. (1989) 'Beliefs and inferences: a test of a rational-emotive hypothesis. 2: On the prospect of seeing a spider', *Psychological Reports*, 64: 115–23.

Ellis, A. (1991) 'The revised ABCs of RET', *Journal of Rational-Emotive and Cognitive-Behavior Therapy*, 9: 139–72.

6

The Role of Concurrent Beliefs in Emotional Disturbance

by Robin Yapp and Windy Dryden

In this chapter we shall outline an expanded model of a client's belief system which serves to: (1) portray the role of ego disturbance and discomfort disturbance beliefs in *perpetuating* emotional disturbance; (2) validate the necessity for REBT therapists to assess and dispute both ego and discomfort beliefs to assist client progress; (3) suggest a possible explanation for why clients may revert to irrational thinking once they have acquired intellectual and emotional insight; (4) explain why clients may report several disturbed emotions at C, and the implications of this both in terms of assessment of beliefs and treatment strategy.

REBT theory holds that when activating events (As) occur, an individual experiences the result or consequences (Cs) as either helpful or unhelpful towards the achievement of his or her goals. The consequences occur not merely because of the A, but because of the individual's evaluative beliefs (B) about the A. These beliefs are viewed as either rational (healthy and self-helping) or irrational (unhealthy and self-defeating). This is referred to as the ABC model of personality (Ellis, 1994). The REBT therapist uses this model to help clients:

1 learn to identify their self-defeating beliefs (IBs);
2 understand how these irrational beliefs largely contribute to their emotional and behavioural problems;
3 confront and dispute (D) their irrational beliefs forcefully, vigorously and persistently;
4 replace these irrational beliefs with rational beliefs that will in turn lead to more healthy, helpful or functional consequences (otherwise referred to as new effect, E).

Thus, the ABC model helps us to understand the causal nature of clients' problems, and when expanded into the ABCDE model,

This chapter was written by Robin Yapp and Windy Dryden and originally published in *The Rational Emotive Behaviour Therapist*, 1995, 3(1): 20–33.

provides the therapist with a step-by-step guide to helping clients overcome their emotional and behavioural problems.

Application of the ABC Model

The ABC model is taught to an ever-increasing number of therapists and clients around the world, and in one of its most basic forms is depicted as follows:

A = activating event
IB = irrational belief about the event (either ego or discomfort disturbance) leading to
C = unhelpful consequence

This superficially simple model has proven to be a valuable formula for both therapist and client. It is easily remembered and can be quickly applied to virtually all cognitive, emotive and behavioural problems. As humans have a tendency to evaluate practically everything (including their thoughts, feelings and behaviours) (Ellis, 1980), this model can be extended according to the type of problem currently being assessed.

Sequential Beliefs: the ABC Model Applied to Secondary Disturbance

The most common use of the extended model is to help identify and explain the role of irrational beliefs when a client suffers from secondary disturbance. For example, a man may be anxious (C2) about feeling depressed (C1). This secondary disturbance results from a *disturbance about disturbance chain*: a process which represents two ABC constructs, one *following on* from the other rather than existing at the same time.

The first ABC construct in the disturbed episode can be depicted as A1 × IB1 = C1 (in this case C1 = depression). This depression (or one of its cognitive or behavioural components) is taken to be a new A (A2), and begins a second ABC construct A2 × IB2 = C2 (C2 = anxiety). If unaddressed, the secondary problem will often be an impediment to progress on the primary target problem. The REBT therapist will normally help the client change the B2 cognitions, before working on changing B1, unless this is contraindicated (Dryden and Yankura, 1993). In more complex permutations of this model – where several ABCs are linked together – the therapist adopts an alternative strategy of targeting the first IB (B1) in the chain. This effectively 'cancels out' the generation of subsequent irrational beliefs (B2, B3, B4, etc.) in the disturbed episode. (For further information on the different types of disturbance chains and recommended treatment strategies see Dryden, 1991.)

Within each of the generated ABC constructs, the IB is held to be *either* an ego disturbance *or* a discomfort disturbance belief (Ellis, 1979, 1980). These two classifications of irrational beliefs are summarized below.

EGO DISTURBANCE

When an individual suffers from ego disturbance she imposes demands on three areas: the self, others, and the world. When these demands are not fulfilled in the past, present or future, the individual damns her whole self. Thus the client may see herself as totally bad, totally worthless or a complete failure. According to REBT theory, ego disturbance is irrational on the grounds that:

(a) an individual is a complex ever-changing process. The traits by which the person can be rated are very likely to change from moment to moment. No matter how many traits of a person are known and used for global self-rating, it is impossible to discover all of that person's characteristics and use them to arrive at a single accurate universal rating.

(b) ego disturbance beliefs are conditional and definitional. To attempt to measure the self-value it is necessary to have a criterion against which the assessment can be made. Any such criterion may be susceptible to change, and the decision of what is a suitable criterion is questionable. What one person maintains is good, another person may view as bad.

(c) the consequences of maintaining ego disturbance are likely to interfere with, or block the achievement of the individual's goals.

For a more comprehensive analysis of the reasons why ego disturbance beliefs are irrational see Dryden (1990).

DISCOMFORT DISTURBANCE

When an individual suffers from discomfort disturbance she also imposes demands in three areas: the self, others, and the world. In contrast to ego disturbance these demands are related to the idea that comfort and comfortable life conditions *must* exist. When these absolute demands are not fulfilled in the past, present or future, the individual views this as awful or unbearable and becomes disturbed. Discomfort disturbance is viewed as irrational mainly because:

Premise	Ego disturbance	Discomfort disturbance
I must	1	4
You must	2	5
Life conditions must	3	6

Figure 6.1 *Disturbance matrix*

- uncomfortable conditions do exist, despite any demands to the contrary;
- uncomfortable conditions may be bad, but they are never *more* than bad;
- all uncomfortable conditions can be endured (however painful this may be) until death occurs;
- the consequences of maintaining discomfort disturbance beliefs are likely to interfere with, or block the achievement of the individual's goals.

There are six possible classifications of these ego or discomfort beliefs as identified by Dryden's disturbance matrix (Dryden and Gordon, 1990); see Figure 6.1.

The REBT therapist teaches the client how to dispute the specific irrational belief that is identified in each ABC. Here an important distinction is to be noted. Disputes designed to target ego disturbance will not fully address discomfort disturbance beliefs. In normal practice this is generally sufficient for most clients, as the client only requires the ability to dispute the identified irrational beliefs for the problem in question. Each individual ABC construct is assessed, brought to the attention of the client and disputed.

On occasion, when a client has one or more ABCs that conform to one category (e.g. an ego disturbance belief in ABC1, and/or ABC2, etc.) and she correctly, forcefully and repeatedly challenges her IB, she may fail to achieve productive change. This failure may be due to a number of factors, for example:

- The client reports that she truly accepts herself, but still has an underlying reservation about how others may see and judge her.
- The client has a (sequential) secondary, or tertiary disturbance belief.

Concurrent Beliefs

We suggest that one further reason for the failure of the above-mentioned client is due to the existence of a *concurrent* irrational

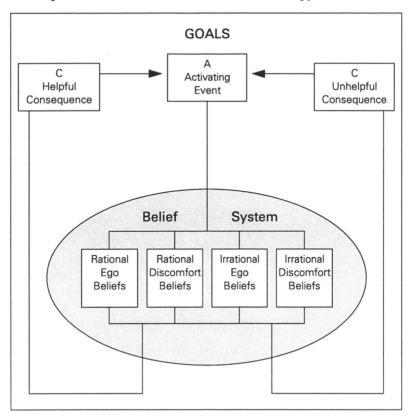

Figure 6.2   *The role of ego and discomfort beliefs within the ABC model*

belief that is contained within the client's belief structure. The con-current irrational belief is from the alternate disturbance category to the disputed irrational belief. For example, where ego disturbance is operative, the alternate category is discomfort disturbance. The presence of the concurrent belief can be explained by opening up and examining the basic ABC model in closer detail. This has been done in Figure 6.2.

In brief, Figure 6.2 shows that the activating event at A triggers the client's belief system (contained within the ellipse). If the A is evaluated rationally in the belief system (B), this will lead to a helpful consequence (C). If the A is evaluated irrationally at B, then this will lead to an unhelpful C. Both helpful and unhelpful Cs may be evaluated as further As, and the cycle or 'loop' repeats to produce secondary disturbances, and so on. All of the aforementioned activity is carried out within the context of the client's goals.

The important distinction this figure illustrates is contained within the belief structure. REBT theory maintains that people can hold elements of a rational belief and an irrational belief about activating events *at the same time* (Dryden, 1990). For example a client may believe 'I want to perform well', and concurrently believe 'because I want to perform well, I *must* do so'. When a client is disturbed, the irrational belief is dominant in the ABC framework. The rational belief is also active, but its effect is cancelled out by the more strongly held irrational belief. If we are able to classify irrational beliefs as either ego or discomfort, it logically follows that this distinction can be applied to their rational counterparts. Thus, at point B we have at least four beliefs operating and existing simultaneously:

1   rational ego beliefs
2   rational discomfort beliefs
3   irrational ego beliefs (ego disturbance)
4   irrational discomfort beliefs (discomfort disturbance)

For the purpose of this model, each of these four beliefs can be classified according to their level of activity as follows:

Dominant-active: the most powerfully held belief that is operative within the client's belief structure – triggered by the critical A;
Concealed-active: a belief that is simultaneously acting to create the same type of emotional consequence but is held less strongly and its effect is masked by the presence of the dominant belief;
Passive: a belief that is operational but has little or no effect on the consequence as it is held very weakly.

It may be useful at this juncture to illustrate this model with an example. Let's suppose that a student has unhelpful feelings of anxiety when faced with the prospect of taking an important examination:

A = prospect of taking an important examination
C = feelings of anxiety

Student's belief structure

IB dominant-active: I must perform perfectly and pass this examination or I am a no-good louse (ego disturbance);
IB concealed-active: My life must not change in any undesirable way as a result of my performance, I couldn't stand it if it did (discomfort disturbance);

RB passive: I would like to perform perfectly and pass this examination but I don't have to. If I do make a mistake it does not mean I am a louse but simply someone who did not perform well on this occasion (rational ego);

RB passive: If my life does change in an undesirable way due to my performance, this will be unfortunate but not unbearable (rational discomfort).

Implications for Practice

By viewing the ABC model in these terms rather than as a single 'B' ABC model, we suggest the implications for clinical practice are as follows.

The therapist may help the client uncover and successfully challenge the dominant IB that is operative in the ABC cycle. Once this dominant IB has been effectively challenged and thereby held lightly, the client's concealed-active IB (as yet unchallenged) is no longer overshadowed and moves up the hierarchy one level to become dominant. Consequently the client's unhelpful feelings of anxiety remain – the *same consequence* is experienced by the client, but the antecedent is a *different* IB.

Self Re-indoctrination of Irrational Beliefs

Ego and discomfort disturbance beliefs both stem from (and contain) the *must*. If the irrational belief is not properly disputed with a full preferential statement (Brian Kelly, personal communication, 1992), the client will have a tendency to re-indoctrinate himself with a musturbatory philosophy.

A full preferential statement (FPS) is where the client states his rational preference and negates his musturbatory demand e.g.: 'I *want* to perform perfectly and pass this examination *but I don't have to*'. Each time the client applies the FPS he is less likely to jump from his preference to a demand, due to the negation of his demand: '*but I don't have to*'.

If the FPS is not used, the client is likely to revert to irrational thinking. For example, in the above case the student believes 'I must perform perfectly and pass this examination or I am a no-good louse.' Once this dominant-active belief has been disputed the client possesses a degree of insight and skill in countering demandingness and self-rating. His concealed-active IB contains a demand in the form of 'My life must not change' and a low frustration tolerance derivative 'I couldn't stand it'. If the client is aware of the concealed-active demand and applies the learned FPS mentioned above to dispute it, the concealed active irrational demand is negated. However, the client would also need to be educated in how to dispute the derivative 'I couldn't stand it'. If the client does not possess LFT disputing skills he is likely to believe 'because I couldn't stand it . . . it absolutely must not be', and continue to be disturbed. To effect a helpful change in the client, it is therefore necessary to:

1 help the client to change the dominant IB – whichever is currently operative;
2 check for the existence of any concealed-active IBs in the alternative modality that may be triggered by the same activating event;
3 help the client identify and dispute this concealed-active belief through standard REBT methods.

As the example demonstrates, the REBT therapist will need to be vigilant in detecting both ego disturbance *and* discomfort disturbance beliefs (dominant-active and concealed-active) within each ABC construct.

Assessing C: Understanding Discrete Emotions, Meta-Emotions, Emotional Blends and Emotional Clusters

The singular ABC model assumes the existence of one activating event, one belief, and one emotional consequence. We have already established the existence of concurrent beliefs, thereby expanding the B to four possible elements, and C to two possible simultaneous disturbed emotional responses.

In this next section we shall use the model of concurrent beliefs to help guide the practitioner by (1) classifying the types of emotional responses at C; (2) explaining why clients may report several disturbed emotions at C; and (3) highlighting the implications of this both in terms of assessment of beliefs and treatment strategy.

In order to classify emotional responses REBT takes the physiological and psychological themes of each emotional episode within the context of A and G (goals), and names this as a discrete emotional response, e.g. 'anxiety', 'anger', 'guilt', 'depression', 'jealousy', 'envy', etc. However, determining these discrete emotions can be problematic. For example, if a male client is about to ask an attractive female for a date in a crowded bar, he may experience two discrete emotions: unhealthy anxiety and unhealthy shame. The consequences of such emotions may include:

Anxiety: overestimates negative features of the threat;
         creates an even more negative threat in his mind
Shame: overestimates the degree of disapproval he will receive.

The above cognitive consequences of holding irrational beliefs (taken from Dryden, 1995) share a similar relationship: they each exaggerate the negative result of experiencing A. In addition, the action tendency of each emotion can be to avoid, withdraw from, or prevent the A from occurring. Physiological responses may also be similar: when a client is anxious or embarrassed he may experience tension, rapid heartbeat, dry mouth, hot flushes and physical discomfort.

As the inferences, beliefs and consequences share similar qualities, it is possible for the therapist to make errors in assessment, e.g. believing the client is experiencing one discrete emotion of anxiety rather than two emotions (anxiety and shame). In practice, during initial assessment, the REBT therapist helps the client to identify and name the unhealthy feeling experienced at C. In most cases clients will report one or more emotional disturbances, for example:

(a) 'I felt anxious', or
(b) 'I felt anxious and then I felt depressed'.

The sequential ABC model proves to be a useful conceptual framework for understanding the origins of each emotional response detailed above. In (a) the client reports a single emotion, fitting neatly into the single ABC construct. In (b) the client expresses the emotions in sequence, suggesting that the client has a meta-emotional problem (in this case secondary disturbance) about the original emotional problem, i.e. depression about his anxiety. However, it is not uncommon for clients to report that at C they experience several different feelings *at the same time*. We shall refer to the simultaneous experience of two emotions as an *emotional blend*, and simultaneous experience of three or more emotions as an *emotional cluster*. For example:

(a) I feel afraid/angry (emotional blend);
(b) I feel so depressed, angry and hurt (emotional cluster).

The existence of concurrent beliefs in the ABC model helps us to understand why both emotional blends and emotional clusters may occur and highlights implications for practice. First, we have already established that a client will have at least four elements of beliefs operational at any one time. In cases where an emotional blend is present, the client may have a single dominant-active irrational belief triggering ego anxiety, and another concurrent irrational belief triggering discomfort anger. As the emotions appear to happen 'simultaneously', the client blends them together and reports both emotions as one. When the therapist attempts to clarify the emotion, the client is likely to choose the consequence resulting from the dominant belief as this is most strongly felt.

In the case of emotional clusters, the client may have *several* concurrent ego or discomfort disturbance beliefs triggered by the actual event. As these emotions are simultaneously triggered, the client attempts to describe the experience, but due to lack of insight or limitations of language will report individual or blended emotions (it can be difficult for the client to report emotional clusters spontaneously, even when asked to). For example, the emotional cluster (b) described above included three emotions and therefore we maintain that three concurrent irrational beliefs existed, triggered by the same actual event, e.g:

Actual event = rejected by partner
1 = I can't stand the thought of living without him (discomfort depression);
2 = He should not have done this to me, and because he has he's no good (ego – anger);
3 = I don't deserve to be treated in this way, he should not have done this to me (ego – hurt);
C = emotional cluster of depression–anger–hurt.

Both an emotional blend and an emotional cluster represent potential dilemmas for the therapist, posing the question 'Which emotion is the C that I need to work with?' It is likely that in such cases the novice therapist would probe for the first most strongly felt emotion and work with this. For example, if the strongest feeling articulated by the client is 'hurt', then this emotion is teased out from the cluster, the others disregarded, and inference chaining commenced. More experienced therapists may regard the depression and anger in the emotional cluster as possible meta-emotions, and probe to establish the client's sequence of ABC constructs. For example the therapist may ask the client: 'How do you feel about being hurt in this way?' If the client does not report the depression or anger as a meta-emotion, or reveals a new meta-emotion (e.g. shame about being hurt), then the initial depression and anger components of the emotional cluster may be assumed to be:

1 elements of the 'hurt' described by the client (as discrete emotional responses can overlap);
2 inaccurate descriptions of healthy responses; or
3 irrelevant, and consequently disregarded.

When this happens the therapist will have inadvertently bypassed irrational beliefs operative in the client's belief system. In the example above this was two IBs. Although the therapist may help the client address the irrational belief leading to the disturbed 'hurt', the client may still fail to recognize and dispute the remaining IBs and thus perpetuate her disturbance. A further point worthy of mention is that if the client perceives that the therapist has disregarded her angry and depressed feelings, then she may evaluate the therapist as either insensitive or incompetent and may withdraw from therapy.

In order to help clients deal with disturbed emotional blends and emotional clusters, we suggest that the therapist will need to be vigilant in assessing C and detect each of the concurrent inferences and beliefs triggered by the A and help the client dispute these. The components of the emotional blend/cluster will be tackled in an order negotiated between the therapist and the client. Two factors will largely determine the outcome of this negotiation process:

- the severity of the disturbance (most strongly felt by the client);
- client's choice versus the most serious problem from a clinical perspective.

For example, if the client reports the emotional cluster of feeling 'angry–hurt–depressed' but when questioned she says 'I feel mostly angry', then this is agreed as the problem to deal with first. The next strongly held feeling (e.g. hurt) is then identified as the second problem, and so on. However, if the therapist discovers that the client has suicidal thoughts arising as part of the depression component (originally agreed as the third problem to address), then from a clinical perspective it would be important to provide the client with a rationale about why this problem is best dealt with first. Ultimately, to preserve the working alliance, it will be necessary to address each component of the emotional blend or emotional cluster in the order that the client chooses.

Human Tendency to 'Backslide'

REBT therapists teach clients to change their irrational beliefs to rational beliefs. The expanded ABC model outlined in this chapter suggests that it is the client's conviction in the 'truth and validity' of the operative belief that will determine the response. If this model is accurate, then the disturbed client is operating on all four elements of the belief system at once (rational ego, rational discomfort, irrational ego, irrational discomfort), but only one of these is dominant – the irrational belief that is held most strongly. The client does not change the core irrational belief, but 'transfers' his fundamental *conviction* in the irrational philosophy to the more rational and healthy alternative. Once this is achieved, the irrational belief then assumes a passive role (as it is weakly held). Because the irrational philosophy is constantly present, rather than completely removed, this may explain why a client who has successfully disputed his irrational beliefs can 'backslide'.

The moment his rational belief is brought into question and held lightly (e.g. in the face of a profound A), the ever-present irrational belief, previously passive, becomes dominant. For example, when a partner dies the client may lightly believe 'I would prefer this not to have happened', but strongly believe 'This absolutely should not have occurred.' If the client had previously disputed all his irrational beliefs and replaced these with rational ones, then the client's belief system would not contain any irrational philosophy. REBT holds that an individual can never be perfect, not even completely rational. If a client was completely rational and had no passive irrational tendencies, then he would not be able to revert to irrational thinking because this would be outside the scope of his belief system.

In practice, highlighting the distinction drawn between changing the irrational belief and transferring the client's conviction in the operative belief may not be necessary. Teaching clients to *transfer* their convictions rather than *change* beliefs is probably a more accurate description of what is required for healthy change, but is also a more complex concept for clients to grasp. The majority of clients will identify with the idea that if something does not work then it will need to be changed. Advising them not to change but to transfer their conviction would probably lead to confusion.

Ellis (1994) maintains that the goal of REBT is to help people become more, but not completely rational. The continued existence of the four belief types (rational and irrational, ego and discomfort) after the disputing process (rather than the removal of irrational beliefs) is theoretically consistent with this aim. Due to the continuing presence of an irrational tendency in his belief system, in order to prevent 'backsliding' the client will need to act on rational insight number three: the need to dispute irrational beliefs forcefully, vigorously and *persistently* – for the rest of his life.

Conclusion

In summary, the existence of concurrent beliefs adds to the evidence (Ellis, 1994) that the ABC model is extremely complex. Using the construct of concurrent irrational beliefs, it has been shown that:

- at least four beliefs will be operating in an ABC construct, and two disturbed Cs may be present;
- two or more simultaneous emotional responses (emotional blends and emotional clusters) may be contained within one ABC construct, rather than existing as a sequence of emotional responses;
- failure to target each concurrent belief (both ego disturbance and discomfort disturbance) may result in the client continuing to disturb herself;
- failure to assess the reported C correctly may lead to the therapist inadvertently missing irrational beliefs held by the client that are relevant to the target problem.

These issues suggest that if the therapist is to help the client effectively, then he or she will need to pay particular attention to accurately assessing the client's reported C, and adopt a comprehensive approach to teaching disputing skills to clients to counter demandingness, awfulizing, low frustration tolerance and self/other rating.

References

Dryden, W. (ed.) (1990) *The Essential Albert Ellis: Seminal Writings on Psychotherapy*. New York: Springer.

Dryden, W. (1991) *Reason and Therapeutic Change*. London: Whurr.

Dryden, W. (1992) *The Incredible Sulk*. London: Sheldon.

Dryden, W. (1995) *Preparing for Client Change in Rational Emotive Behaviour Therapy*. London: Whurr.

Dryden, W. and Gordon, J. (1990) *What is Rational-Emotive Therapy? A Personal and Practical Guide*. Essex: Gale Centre Publications.

Dryden, W. and Yankura, J. (1993) *Counselling Individuals: A Rational-Emotive Handbook*, 2nd edn. London: Whurr.

Ellis, A. (1979) 'Discomfort anxiety: part 1. A new cognitive behavioral construct', *Rational Living*, 14(2): 3–8.

Ellis, A. (1980) 'Discomfort anxiety: part 2. A new cognitive behavioral construct', *Rational Living*, 15(1): 25–30.

Ellis, A. (1994) *Reason and Emotion in Psychotherapy: Revised and Updated*. New York: Birch Lane Press.

7

Who is Suitable for Brief REBT?

There is much debate in the brief therapy literature concerning who is suitable for brief intervention. Some theorists (see Davanloo, 1978) argue in favour of stringent inclusion criteria while others (e.g. Budman and Gurman, 1988) are more liberal in their views on who is suitable for brief therapeutic intervention. In this chapter I will outline my views on the question: who is suitable for brief REBT? My approach to brief REBT is based on an 11-session protocol which I discuss in Dryden (1995).

Suitability Criteria

In my view, there are seven indications that a person seeking help will benefit from brief REBT.

The person is able and willing to present her problems in a specific form and set goals that are concrete and achievable.

It often occurs that at the outset people seeking therapeutic help talk about their problems in vague, abstract terms. Your task as a brief REBT therapist is to help them as quickly as possible to translate these abstractions into specific problem statements. You will be able to do so with most people, but a minority will be either unable or unwilling to discuss their problems or goals in a concrete form. If the person is able to specify her problems and goals, but is not willing to do so, perhaps because she doesn't think it would be helpful to do so, then this person is not a good candidate for brief REBT or even longer-term REBT. In such instances it is useful to discover what she thinks will be therapeutic for her and then make a relevant referral.

When a person appears unable to discuss her problems and goals in concrete terms, she is also not a good candidate for brief REBT, but may do better in longer-term REBT, where you may be able to train her to be specific. You need to be cautious here, however, as some individuals have cognitive deficits which prevent them from

This chapter was originally published in *The Rational Emotive Behaviour Therapist*, 1995, 3(1): 39–44.

being concrete. If you suspect that this is the case you may wish to refer the person for a neuropsychological assessment in the first instance.

The person's problems are of the type that can be dealt with in 11 sessions.

In my opinion, brief REBT is indicated when the person's problems are not severe. They may 'feel' severe to the person, but this is not what I am referring to. By the term 'severe' I am talking about problems that are chronic (i.e. not of recent onset) *and* that significantly disrupt the person's life. It is the presence of both of these problem characteristics that, for me, contraindicate brief REBT. It may well be that a person may have a chronic problem that does not significantly disrupt the person's life or he may have a significantly disruptive problem that is acute (i.e. of recent origin). By themselves, these problems are not contraindications for brief REBT. However, like all forms of brief therapy, brief REBT works best when the person's problems are not in the severe range.

It is important to recognize that the person seeking help may come to therapy with a number of problems, some severe and some not. The person may be a good candidate for brief REBT if he is prepared to target his less severe problems for intervention *and* the existence of his severe problems does not prevent him from doing so. However, unsurprisingly, more often he will wish immediate help for his severe problems. In this case, longer-term REBT should be offered instead of brief treatment.

The person is able and willing to target two problems that she particularly wants to work on during therapy.

It is as important to realize the limitations of brief REBT as it is to appreciate its strengths. One of its limitations is that, in all probability, you will not have the time to deal with all of your client's problems in depth. My view is that in 11 sessions you only have time to deal with two of your client's problems in depth, while perhaps having the time to see the linking themes across her problems and doing *some* work on the *core* irrational beliefs that underpin these problems. Given this, if the person seeking help cannot, for whatever reason, limit herself to working on two target problems, then brief REBT is not the modality of choice for her and longer-term REBT should be considered. I should add that if the person targets only one problem for change, then brief REBT is indicated. She doesn't have to target exactly two target problems. One will do!

The person has understood the ABCDEs of REBT and has indicated that this way of conceptualizing and dealing with her problems makes sense and is potentially helpful to her.

REBT is based on a specific model of psychological disturbance and its remediation. It is important that the person seeking help understand the nature of this model so that she can make an informed decision on whether or not to commit herself to brief REBT. This is why it is important to explain the REBT model of psychological problems and their treatment in the first session. This is done by teaching your client the ABCDEs of REBT. If your client has understood this model and thinks that this way of conceptualizing and dealing with her problems makes sense and is potentially helpful to her, then this is a good sign that she may benefit from brief REBT.

If she thinks that it is not relevant to her problems and/or not useful then this is a contraindication for brief REBT. If the person is undecided about the potential relevance and utility to her problems, then you need to address this issue more fully before asking her to commit herself to brief REBT.

The person has understood the therapist's tasks and her own tasks in brief REBT, has indicated that these seem potentially useful to her and is willing to carry out her tasks.

Various codes of professional ethics stipulate that a person seeking help has to give informed consent before the therapist uses a therapeutic intervention. In brief REBT, we take this seriously by explaining in the first or second session what our tasks are as brief REBT therapists and what we consider our clients' tasks to be. This, of course, has to be explained in terms that clients can understand. Your client is a good candidate for brief REBT in this respect if she understood your respective therapeutic tasks, has given some indication that she believes that these tasks may be useful to her and she has said that she is willing to carry out her tasks.

You need to take care in forming your opinion of your client's suitability for brief REBT on this criterion. For example, your client may say that she understands what you both need to do to make brief REBT effective, but she may think that these tasks will not be helpful to her. Or she may understand the tasks, see their potential utility, but not be prepared to carry them out, hoping that you will do the work for her. It is important to explore and respond constructively to any doubts and reservations that she may have about the task domain of REBT. This may involve correcting any misconceptions that she may have about this approach to therapy. Finally, it is advisable to form an opinion concerning whether or not the person seeking help has the ability to put her therapeutic tasks into practice. If you judge that she does not, then effect a suitable referral.

The person's level of functioning in her everyday life is sufficiently high to enable her to carry out her tasks both inside and outside therapy sessions.

Most proponents of brief therapy recognize that this approach works better with clients who are functioning relatively well in life (see Davanloo, 1978). Consequently, my view is that it is best to offer brief work to this clinical population. I do not go along with the view that is sometimes expressed that brief therapy can be offered to everybody because all will gain *something* from this approach. I believe in tailoring the therapy modality to the person rather than offering everyone a single modality (Dryden, 1993). You need to make a judgement concerning whether or not your client is functioning sufficiently well in life to respond productively to brief REBT. This can be done in a number of ways.

First, as various authorities advocate (e.g. Malan, 1980), you can carry out a thorough formal assessment of the person's level of psychological functioning or arrange for someone to do this for you. Some therapy agencies have an intake interview policy where everyone seeking help receives an assessment-oriented intake interview with someone who will not become the person's therapist, but will refer the person to a therapist if he or she judges that the person is suitable for brief therapy.

Secondly, you can rely on the judgement of an external referral agent. Many of my referrals come from psychiatrists who carry out a full mental status examination and take a full history from the people that they refer to me. A full report invariably accompanies the referral. In the vast majority of cases where they have referred to my brief therapy practice, I have found their judgements to be accurate. This is also true of a smaller number of general practitioners who refer to my brief therapy practice.

Thirdly, in the absence of a full report on the person's level of psychological functioning from someone whose judgement you trust, and when you do not yourself carry out such a full assessment, you may decide to assume that the person is healthy enough to be suitable for brief REBT unless and until you have evidence to the contrary. If and when you gain such evidence, you will decide to refer the person to a more suitable treatment modality. For reasons discussed earlier, I do not agree with this approach. I prefer to make a judgement myself that the person is suitable for brief REBT or rely on the judgement of someone whose opinion I trust than make the assumption, on limited information, that the person is suitable for brief REBT until proven otherwise.

There is early evidence that a good working bond can be developed between you and the person seeking help.

My approach to brief REBT described in Dryden (1995) lasts for 11 sessions. Given this, it is important that you are able to develop a good working bond very early in therapy. On this criterion, a person is a good candidate for brief REBT when she is able to discuss her problems openly with you and a good rapport develops between the two of you. However, if in the first session the person is very reticent and there seems to be an antipathy between the two of you that cannot easily be remedied, then the person is not a good candidate for brief REBT, at least with you as her therapist. If this occurs, it is sensible for you to make a suitable referral.

Contraindications for Brief REBT

Having described the seven indications that suggest that a person is suitable for brief REBT, let me consider the contraindications for brief therapy. While there is no definitive answer to this question in the brief REBT field, my view is that if any of the following conditions exist, I will not offer the person a contract for brief therapy:

- the person is antagonistic to the REBT view of psychological disturbance and its remediation;
- the person disagrees with the therapeutic tasks that REBT outlines for both therapist and client;
- the person is unable to carry out the tasks of a client in brief REBT;
- the person is at present seriously disturbed and has a long history of such disturbance;
- the person seeking help and the therapist are clearly a poor therapeutic match; and
- the person's problems are vague and amorphous and cannot be specified even with the therapist's help.

Between the definite indications and contraindications for brief REBT lies the grey area where a person may meet some of the indications for brief REBT, but not others. As long as the person does not meet any of the contraindications listed above, the only guidance I can give is that the greater the number of indications present, the more likely it is that the person is suitable for brief

REBT. It is useful to discuss cases that fall into the grey area with your supervisor.

The other factor to take into account is the client's actual response to brief REBT. This cannot be known until you have begun therapy, but a person may meet all the suitability criteria that I have outlined yet still respond poorly to REBT.

The reverse is also true. I have occasionally taken the risk and offered a person who has met few of the indications for brief REBT (but none of the contraindications) a brief therapy contract and have been pleasantly surprised at his positive response. My view concerning the client's response to brief REBT has been put succinctly by Budman and Gurman (1988: 25):

> Our recommendations in patient selection are to monitor the patient's response to treatment on a trial basis; to be prepared to make creative modifications as necessary (two such modifications may involve the patient's seeing another therapist or including the patient's family) and to be prepared to use various alternatives, including longer and more open-ended treatment.

I would only add one thing to this statement. Be aware of and do not exceed your own limitations. Thus, if you consider that involving a client's family would be a helpful, creative modification, but you do not have the skills to do this, either refer the case to an REBT therapist with expertise in family work or involve such a therapist in the family sessions as a co-therapist.

References

Budman, S.H. and Gurman, A.S. (1988) *Theory and Practice of Brief Therapy*. New York: Guilford.

Davanloo, H. (ed.) (1978) *Basic Principles and Techniques in Short-Term Dynamic Psychotherapy*. New York: SP Medical and Scientific Books.

Dryden, W. (1993) *Reflections on Counselling*. London: Whurr.

Dryden, W. (1995) *Brief Rational Emotive Behaviour Therapy*. Chichester: Wiley.

Malan, D.H. (1980) 'Criteria for selection', in H. Davanloo (ed.), *Short-Term Dynamic Psychotherapy*. New York: Jason Aronson.

8

Paradoxical REBT: A Humorous Intervention

The use of humour in REBT has been well documented. For example, Albert Ellis (1987) has written on the use of rational humorous songs and I have noted that brief humorous interventions, including where the therapist does something funny in the session, are often effective in encouraging clients to take themselves and their problems seriously, but not too seriously (Dryden, 1986). Most REBT therapists with whom I have discussed this issue consider that humour, while effective, should not dominate the therapeutic proceedings. While this is sound advice, I have found that with certain clients the extended use of what I call paradoxical REBT is particularly helpful. These are clients who have a keen sense of humour themselves and can appreciate the therapist's use of humorous irony. Before I discuss and illustrate paradoxical REBT, I will state the rather obvious point that its use depends on the client and therapist having already established a strong working alliance.

What Is Paradoxical REBT?

A therapist is practising paradoxical REBT when she adopts, for an extended period of time, a *reductio ad absurdum* stance towards her client. Here the therapist does not challenge any of the client's irrational beliefs; rather, she not only agrees with these irrational beliefs, but exaggerates them in a way that is subtly humorous and overtly ironic. The following example will make this clear.

The Case of Gerry

Gerry is a client of mine who has grandiose demands of himself, others and the world. He believes that he must always fulfil himself and that others must give him what he deserves. Furthermore, Gerry believes that life conditions must be easy or exciting depending upon which demand is predominant at the time. Gerry has been successful at using standard or non-paradoxical REBT with himself when he

This chapter was originally published in *The Rational Emotive Behaviour Therapist*, 1994, 2(2): 76–9.

chooses to employ it, but gets bored after his initial burst of enthusiasm wears off. Gerry has a very good sense of humour and appreciates irony and is thus a good candidate for paradoxical REBT. The following dialogue which initially follows a non-paradoxical line took place in the course of a telephone session.

> *Gerry*: I've been using disputing with myself but it's been tough going recently.
> *Windy*: And how have you responded to the toughness?
> *Gerry*: I've tended to give up of late.
> *Windy*: Why?
> *Gerry*: Because the disputing should still be exciting.
> *Windy*: Why do you think it should?
> *Gerry*: Because I deserve it.

> [*I now decide to take a paradoxical stance with Gerry.*]

> *Windy*: Of course you do. How could I think otherwise?
> *Gerry*: [*laughs*] So why won't the world give me the excitement that I crave?
> *Windy*: Beats me. That lousy world for depriving a doll like you.
> *Gerry*: And another thing. There's a woman that I've had my eye on, but I shouldn't have to chase her.
> *Windy*: Of course you shouldn't. To even think of such a thing is a heresy. She should chase you. After all, that's the least you deserve.
> *Gerry*: [*laughs*] You're right. In fact, she should not only chase me, but she should also allow me to go off with other women when I want to and not complain about it.

> [*It is clear to me that by now Gerry is well aware of my ironic, paradoxical stance and is joining me by exaggerating his own grandiosity. In doing so he is poking fun at his own grandiose ideas and, I would venture, is disputing them in the process.*]

> *Windy*: Of course she should. She should be grateful that you would even deign to look at her – and the very thought of her daring to complain about you going after other women. The very idea! Surely she knows that she was put on to this earth just to give you pleasure.
> *Gerry*: [*convulsed with laughter*] Yeah, that's right.
> *Windy*: Now we have to stop in a moment, although the fact that you have agreed to have me as your therapist makes me want to choke on those words. I realize that I should be at your beck and call morning, noon and night, but I am getting on a bit, so you'll have to forgive me.
> *Gerry*: [*laughs*] Agreed.
> *Windy*: Now, how about as a homework assignment, you remind yourself of all the reasons why the world and other people should give you exactly what you want when you want it.
> *Gerry*: That sounds a good idea.
> *Windy*: Although, now I think of it why don't I do that for you. Yes, that's it. I'll do the homework for you and you will get the benefit

from it. That's the least I can do for such a deserving person as yourself.

Gerry: All right, I get your point. But I think this way of disputing my beliefs is very good and will be a good alternative at times to the standard stuff.

What Gerry has just done is important and confirms my original hunch that he would be a good candidate for paradoxical REBT. He has just shown that he is able to stand back from our paradoxical work and see it for what it is – a useful alternative to standard REBT. He also sees it as an additional way of disputing his irrational beliefs between sessions. If he was unable to step back from the paradoxical dialogue and resume a non-paradoxical discussion fairly quickly, he would not be a good candidate for paradoxical work. In addition, if he became histrionic during the paradoxical work, this would be another contraindication for this kind of work. Furthermore, if Gerry either believed that I was serious or thought I was being unhelpfully sarcastic, then I would have stopped immediately and resumed a standard, non-paradoxical REBT approach with him.

The successful use of paradoxical REBT involves the development of a tacit understanding between therapist and client that the therapist is on the client's side and that she is being helpful by being paradoxical. For clients who can see this, who have a healthy ironic sense of the absurd and can join in the spirit of the work, paradoxical REBT can be very therapeutic. For other clients, it should be used sparingly, if at all.

References

Dryden, W. (1986) 'Vivid RET', in A. Ellis and R. Grieger (eds), *Handbook of Rational-Emotive Therapy, Volume 2*, New York: Springer.

Ellis, A. (1987) 'The use of rational humorous songs in psychotherapy', in W.F. Fry, Jr. and W.A. Salameh (eds), *Handbook of Humor in Psychotherapy: Advances in the Clinical Use of Humor*. Sarasota, FL: Professional Resource Exchange.

9

Teaching the Principles of Unconditional Self-Acceptance in a Structured, Group Setting

In this chapter I will describe an eight-week psycho-educational group that I run in which I teach group members the principles of unconditional self-acceptance. These principles stem from the theory of rational emotive behaviour therapy (REBT).

In the chapter, I will: (1) briefly review the concept of ego disturbance in relation to REBT theory; (2) present the principles of unconditional self-acceptance; (3) outline the steps of a self-acceptance group and some of the exercises that I use at each step and discuss briefly the context in which I run these groups.

REBT and Ego Disturbance

Rational emotive behaviour therapy is an approach to counselling and psychotherapy which can be best placed within the cognitive-behavioural psychotherapeutic tradition. One of its basic premises is that psychological disturbance stems primarily from the irrational beliefs that we hold about ourselves, others and the world. However, REBT theory holds that the way we feel, think and act are inter-twined so that when considering their clients' feelings of depression, for example, rational emotive behaviour therapists will consider not only the beliefs that underpin the clients' depression, but also the behaviour which may serve to perpetuate their depressogenic beliefs.

REBT therapists can, in my view, best be seen as psychological educators in that they will teach their clients the basic REBT view of disturbance and once the latter have indicated that they wish to work in this way will teach clients how to identify, challenge and change the irrational beliefs which underpin their psychological problems. For a much fuller consideration of the theory and practice of REBT see Dryden (1995a, 1995b).

Since this chapter concerns a structured, group approach to teaching clients unconditional self-acceptance I will first outline the

---

This chapter was originally published in R. Bayne, I. Horton and J. Bimrose (eds), *New Directions in Counselling*. London: Routledge, 1996.

REBT concept of ego disturbance before presenting the REBT concept of unconditional self-acceptance.

EGO DISTURBANCE

REBT theory distinguishes between two major types of psychological disturbance: ego disturbance and discomfort disturbance (Dryden, 1994). Ego disturbance stems from irrational beliefs related to a person's 'self', while discomfort disturbance stems from irrational beliefs related to that individual's personal domain unrelated to his 'self', but centrally related to his sense of comfort.

Ego disturbance results when a person makes a demand on himself, others, or the world and when that demand is not met the person puts himself down in some way. The following themes are usually involved in ego disturbance:

- failing to achieve an important target or goal;
- acting incompetently (in public or private);
- not living up to one's standards;
- breaking one's ethical code;
- being criticized;
- being ridiculed;
- not being accepted, approved, appreciated or loved by significant others.

Ego-related irrational beliefs are found in a variety of emotional disturbances. Please note, however, that I am not saying that these ego irrational beliefs completely account for the emotions listed below. Rather, I am saying that these beliefs are often found when clients report these emotional experiences. In the following examples, you will note that each of these irrational beliefs contains two elements. First, there is a demanding belief which often takes the form of a 'must', 'absolute should', 'have to' or 'got to'; secondly there is a self-downing belief which takes the form of a global negative evaluation of one's total 'self'. REBT theory states that self-downing beliefs are derived from the musturbatory beliefs.

Depression

'Because I have failed the test, as I absolutely should not have done, I am a failure.'

'Since my partner has rejected me, as he absolutely should not have done, this proves that I am no good.'

Anxiety

'If I fail at my upcoming test, which I must not do, I will be a failure.'

'If he rejects me as I think he will soon, but which he must not do, I will be no good.'

Guilt

'I have hurt the feelings of my parents, which I absolutely should not have done, and therefore am a bad person.'

'I failed to help a good friend of mine. The fact that I did not do what I absolutely should have done proves that I am a rotten person.'

Shame

'I have acted foolishly in front of my peers, which I absolutely should not have done, and this makes me an inadequate person.'

'I have been having sexual feelings towards my sister, which I absolutely should not have, and the fact that I have these feelings makes me a shameful person.'

Hurt

'My ex-boyfriend is going out with my best friend, which absolutely should not happen. Since it is happening, this proves that I am unlovable.'

Anger

'You absolutely should not have criticized me in the way that you did. Your criticism reminds me that I am a failure.'

Jealousy

'If my husband looks at another woman, which he must not do, it means that he finds her more attractive, which must not happen and proves that I am worthless.'

Envy

'My friend is making better progress than I am in our respective careers. I must have what he has and because I don't this makes me less worthy than I would be if I had what he has.'

Unconditional Self-Acceptance

Ego disturbance occurs when a person makes a global negative evaluation of her total self, which in turn is based on the existence of a musturbatory belief. REBT theory states that the healthy alternative to ego disturbance is based on a set of beliefs centred on the concept of unconditional self-acceptance. In this section I will outline the ten principles that underpin this concept.

Human beings cannot legitimately be given a single global rating.

In the previous section I gave several examples of the ways in which people put themselves down (e.g. 'I am a failure', 'I am a bad person'). Each of these involves the person giving himself or herself a single global rating. Indeed, the concept of self-esteem frequently advocated by the majority of counsellors and psychotherapists is based on this same principle. Low self-esteem involves the assignment of a single, negative, global rating to a person, and high self-esteem involves the assignment of a single, positive, global rating to the person.

REBT theory argues that it is not possible to give a person a single global rating, be it negative or positive. This is best shown if we define clearly the terms 'self' and 'esteem'. First, let's take the term 'self'. Paul Hauck has provided a very simple, but profound definition of the self. He says that the self is 'every conceivable thing about you that can be rated' (1991: 33). This means that all your thoughts, images, feelings, behaviours and bodily parts are part of your 'self' and all these different aspects that belong to you from the beginning of your life to the moment just before your death have to be included in your 'self'. Now let's consider the term 'esteem'. This term is derived from the verb to estimate which means to give something a rating, judgement or estimation. The question then arises: can we give the 'self' a single *legitimate* rating, estimation or judgement which completely accounts for its complexity? The answer is clearly 'no'. As Hauck (1991) notes, it is possible to rate different aspects of one's 'self', but a person is far too complex to warrant a single, legitimate, global rating.

Even if it were possible to give a person a single global rating – a task which would involve a team of objective judges and a computer so powerful that it could analyse the millions upon millions of data produced by that person – as soon as that global judgement was made, it would become immediately redundant since that person would continue to produce more data. In other words, a person is an ongoing, ever-changing process and defies the ascription of a single, static, global judgement.

To summarize, it is not possible, in any legitimate sense, to give one's self a single global rating since you are too complex to merit such an evaluation; and you are an ongoing ever-changing process who defies being statically rated by yourself or by others.

By contrast, the concept of unconditional self-acceptance does not involve any such rating or evaluation. However, and this is a crucial point, unconditional self-acceptance does allow you to rate different aspects of yourself. Indeed, it encourages this type of evaluation, since doing so allows you to focus on your negative aspects and do something to improve them without self-blame. Conversely, if you focus on your negative aspects from the standpoint of self-esteem, then you are less likely to change them because you are sidetracked by giving your 'self' a global negative rating for having these aspects. It is difficult to change anything about yourself while you are beating yourself over the head for having those aspects in the first place.

Human beings are essentially fallible.

REBT theory holds that if human beings have an essence it is probably that we are essentially fallible. As Maxie Maultsby (1984) has put it, humans have an incurable error-making tendency. I would add that we frequently make more serious mistakes than we are prepared to accept and that we often keep repeating the same errors. Why do we do this? As Paul Hauck (1991) has put it, we keep repeating our errors out of stupidity, ignorance or because we are psychologically disturbed. Albert Ellis (1994) has noted that humans find it very easy to disturb themselves and difficult to undisturb themselves. Self-acceptance, then, means acknowledging that our essence is fallibility and that we are not perfectible.

All humans are equal in humanity, but unequal in their different aspects.

This principle follows on from the two listed above. If the essence of humanity is fallibility then all humans are equal in their humanity, and since human beings cannot be rated it follows that no human is worthier than any other. This principle reveals rational emotive behaviour therapy as one of the most, if not the most, humanistic of all psychotherapies. However, this principle of parity does not deny that there is a great deal of variation among human beings with respect to their different aspects. Thus, Adolf Hitler may be equal in humanity to Mother Theresa, but in terms of their compassion to human beings, the latter far outscores the former.

The rational use of the concept of human worth.

From the principles discussed thus far, you will see that the concept of human worth is problematic since it rests on the assignment of a single global rating (worth) to a process (the 'self') which defies such a simple rating. However, a number of clients want to retain the idea of human worth even though it has inherent problems. The main problem with the concept is that people normally make their worth contingent on variables that change (e.g. 'I am worthwhile if I do well in my exams', which implies that if I do not do well then I am not worthwhile). Even if a person fulfils the conditions of worth at any given moment, she is still vulnerable to emotional disturbance if those conditions are not continually met.

The only way that a person can apply the concept of human worth in a rational manner is to make her worth contingent on one of two constants. First, she can say that she is worthwhile because she is human. Secondly, she can say that she is worthwhile as long as she is alive. This can even be applied by people who believe in an afterlife ('I am worthwhile as long as I am alive in this life or any future life that I may have'). The difficulty with this concept, as Ellis (1972) has shown, is that someone can just as easily say: 'I am worthless because I am alive' or 'I am worthless because I am human'. For this reason, most REBT therapists discourage their clients from using the concept of human worth.

Unconditional self-acceptance avoids errors of overgeneralization.

When people apply the concept of conditional self-esteem they constantly make errors of overgeneralization, or what might be called part–whole errors. In the part–whole error, a person infers that he has failed to achieve a certain goal (which represents a part of the person), evaluates this failure negatively and then concludes that he (the whole of the person) is a failure. In other words, he rates the whole of himself on the basis of his rating of a part of himself. Applying the concept of unconditional self-acceptance to this example, the person would still infer that he has failed to achieve his goal and would still evaluate this failure negatively. However, his conclusion – that his failure proves that he is a fallible human being – would be perfectly logical.

Unconditional self-acceptance is based on a flexible, preferential philosophy.

Earlier in this chapter I pointed out that self-downing beliefs are derived from rigid, musturbatory beliefs, as in Albert Ellis's memorable phrase: 'Shouldhood leads to shithood. You're never a shit without a should.' What follows from this is that unconditional self-acceptance beliefs are derived from flexible, preferential beliefs. For example, if you believe that you are inadequate because you acted in a socially inappropriate manner then this self-downing belief stems from the rigid belief: 'I must not behave inappropriately in a social context.' A self-accepting alternative belief would involve you accepting yourself as a fallible human being who is not inadequate. This belief in turn would stem from the flexible belief: 'I would prefer not to act in a socially inappropriate manner, but there's no reason why I absolutely must not do so.'

Self-acceptance promotes constructive action, not resignation.

If we can accept ourselves as fallible human beings with all that this means, paradoxically we have a much better chance of minimizing our errors and psychological problems than if we condemn ourselves for having them in the first place. Such acceptance, then, does not imply resignation, as many people think. Rather, it promotes our constructive efforts to learn from our errors and minimize our tendency to disturb ourselves. Self-acceptance does this because, as shown above, it is based on a flexible philosophy of desire, in this case a desire to live as happily as possible. This desire motivates us to take constructive action. Conversely, resignation is based on the idea that there is nothing we can do to improve aspects of ourselves so there is no point in trying. This, then, is the antithesis of self-acceptance.

Unconditional self-acceptance is a habit that can be acquired (but never perfectly, nor for all time).

Behaviour therapists often construe self-defeating behaviour as bad habits that can be broken, and many clients resonate with the idea that self-downing is a bad habit that can be broken. If you want to use the idea of self-downing and unconditional self-acceptance as habits you can do so, but with the following caveats. Be careful to stress that the 'habit' of self-downing can be broken, but never perfectly and not in a once and for all manner. Similarly, stress that unconditional self-acceptance can be acquired, but again never perfectly nor for all time. Emphasize that it is the very nature of fallible human beings to go back to 'self-downing' under stress even though your client may have worked very hard to break this habit. In doing so you are helping your client to accept herself for her lack of self-acceptance!

Internalizing the philosophy of unconditional self-acceptance is difficult and involves hard work.

Understanding the concept of unconditional self-acceptance is not that difficult. Internalizing a philosophy of unconditional self-acceptance so that it makes a positive difference to the way we think, feel and act most certainly is difficult. Here, it is useful to help clients view the acquisition of self-acceptance as similar to the acquisition of any new skill that has to be learned against the background of a well-ingrained habit that has been overlearned (such as golf or tennis). Acquiring self-acceptance will involve your clients in a lot of hard work; work that has to be done even though clients will experience feelings and tendencies to act that are consistent with their more thoroughly ingrained philosophy of self-downing. This means that clients will have to tolerate a period of 'feeling all wrong' as they strive to internalize a philosophy that makes perfect sense, but is not yet believed. Such conviction comes from repeatedly challenging self-downing beliefs and acting in a way that is consistent with self-accepting beliefs.

Self-acceptance requires force and energy.

The hard work mentioned above can be done in two ways. It can be done with force and energy where, for example, clients challenge their self-downing beliefs with a great deal of force and throw themselves into acting in ways that are consistent with their newly acquired self-accepting beliefs. Or it can be done in a weak, 'namby-pamby' fashion. Since people tend to hold their self-downing beliefs quite rigidly, the latter way of trying to acquire a philosophy of self-acceptance will just not work. It is important to help clients understand the importance of meeting strength with strength or fighting fire with fire. Given this, the more clients use force and energy as they strive to accept themselves, the better their results will be.

Running Self-Acceptance Groups

I will begin this section by providing a brief outline of the basic assumption that underpins self-acceptance groups. Then I will describe the context in which I run these groups before providing a session-by-session account of a typical self-acceptance group.

BASIC ASSUMPTION

The self-acceptance groups that I run are based on the idea that the philosophy of self-acceptance can be taught in a structured, educational manner and can be understood by group members in a short period of time. Although internalizing this philosophy is a long and arduous endeavour which takes far longer than the eight-week period over which the group is run, it is possible in this short period to help group members to take the first steps in integrating this philosophy into their belief system.

THE CONTEXT

The context in which a therapy group is run has a decided impact on how it is established and how much impact it has on the well-being of its members. As one colleague complained, 'How can you run a group when every week the chairs are different?' To which I replied, 'Where I work the chairs are the same every week, but the group membership is different!' I work one morning a week in a private hospital setting where two types of group are offered: open groups where people come and go and every week the size and membership of the group is different; and closed groups where the same group of clients meets every week for a time-limited period. The self-acceptance groups to be described here are, in my experience, best run as a closed group. If they were run as an open group, I would have to introduce the same ideas every week and group cohesion would be lost. A closed group means that clients are introduced to the same ideas and the same techniques at the same time, which means that they can help one another in a way that they couldn't if the group were open.

One issue that does need to be addressed if you work in a private hospital is the timing of clients' appointments with their consultant psychiatrists. Unless you inform consultants of the times of your self-acceptance group and elicit their agreement that they will not schedule appointments during this time, then the group will be disrupted by clients coming back from or going out to see their consultants.

FORMING THE GROUP

Before you form the group, you need to make decisions about the size of the group, how often it is to meet and how long each session will be. In a private hospital there is the additional constraint that many clients, once they have become 'day patients', do not attend for long periods of time, unless they can afford the high fees or their insurance cover permits long-term attendance. Consequently, my practice is to run a self-acceptance group weekly for one and a half hours over an an eight-week period. I have found that a group of between seven and nine clients works best (allowing for one dropout per group).

Since my attendance at the hospital is limited to one morning a week, I do not have the time to interview all the people who wish to join the group. I leave the selection of group members to one of the full-time workers at the hospital who know the nature of the group and the types of client who will benefit most from it. These are people whose problems are mainly ego-related and who have had previous exposure to REBT or cognitive therapy and agree with the idea that dysfunctional beliefs are at the core of psychological disturbance. In addition, group members need to commit to weekly attendance over the life of the group and be prepared to put into practice what they learn from the group, which means the regular completion of homework assignments.

A SESSION-BY-SESSION OUTLINE OF A SELF-ACCEPTANCE GROUP

Session 1

Introductions   The members of the group and I introduce ourselves to one another.

Clarifying the preconditions for attendance   Here, I stress that the group is for people whose problems are to do with negative attitudes towards the self and that weekly attendance is expected from all. I also explain the usual rule of confidentiality for group members and elicit members' willingness to comply with this rule.

Who wants high self-esteem   I normally begin a self-acceptance group by asking members who amongst them would like to have high self-esteem (or feel better about themselves). Virtually everyone raises their hands. I then ask each member to indicate what would raise their self-esteem. The kind of answers I get are:

- 'Doing well at work.'
- 'Being a better mother.'
- 'Being loved.'
- 'Living up to my principles.'
- 'Doing voluntary work.'

Teaching the principles of unconditional self-acceptance   Before I deal with the responses to the question, 'What would raise your self-esteem?' I spend most of the first session teaching the ten principles of unconditional self-acceptance outlined in the first half of this chapter. After teaching each point I pause for questions and observations from group members.

Another look at self-esteem   After I have finished teaching the ten principles of self-esteem, I ask the group members to reconsider their answers to my question, 'What would raise your self-esteem?' I help them to see that their responses do not serve to raise their self-esteem, but are desirable things to have or achieve in their own right. I show them that self-esteem is contingent upon doing well at work, being loved, and so on and if they were to do poorly at work later or lose the love of a significant person, for example, their self-esteem would plummet. Helping group members to understand that the concept of self-esteem is the cause of their problems and not the solution is very liberating for most.

Homework   Virtually all the members in my self-acceptance groups have been exposed to REBT or cognitive-behaviour therapy and therefore are familiar with the important role that homework assignments have in the therapeutic process. Since it is beyond the scope of this chapter to deal with cases where group members do not do their homework assignments or modify them in some way, I refer the interested reader to Dryden (1995b).

The first homework assignment I suggest that group members carry out before the second group session is to read Chapters 1 and 3 of Paul Hauck's (1991) book on self-acceptance entitled *Hold Your Head Up High*. Chapter 1 outlines the problems that occur when people do not accept themselves and Chapter 3 presents the principles of self-acceptance. These chapters serve as a reminder of the material covered in the first session. I suggest that while reading the material group members make a note of points that they disagree with or are unsure of for discussion the following week.

Session 2

Reviewing homework   It is an important principle of REBT that if you set a homework assignment then you review it the following session. So at the beginning of this session (and all subsequent sessions) it is important to review what the group members did for homework. In doing so, I correct any misconceptions that group members display in their reading of the chapters in Hauck's book.

Goal-setting   At this point, the group members are ready to consider what they can achieve from the group and what they can't. I point out that my role is to teach them both the principles of self-acceptance and some techniques to help them to begin to internalize this philosophy. What I can do is to help them begin the journey towards self-acceptance. In eight weeks, I cannot help them to complete this journey. Given this, I ask them to set suitable goals for the group. 'What,' I ask, 'will you have achieved by the end of the eight weeks that would show you that you have begun the long and arduous journey towards self-acceptance?' I encourage members to divide into smaller groups and to make their goals as realistic and specific as possible. I then ask one group member to make a written note of everybody's goals, which I then photocopy and distribute at the end of the session so that everybody has a copy of the goals of each member.

Dealing with a specific example of the target problem   I ask group members to choose a specific example of a situation in which they considered themselves to be worthless, inadequate, bad, etc. I then ask each member in turn to talk about the experience briefly to the rest of the group. After the person has finished relating the experience, I use the ABC framework of REBT to help assess it, where A stands for the activating event, B for her musturbatory and self-downing beliefs and C for her major disturbed negative emotion and/or self defeating behaviour.

Homework   For homework, I ask each group member to use the ABC framework to analyse another example of 'low self-esteem'.

Session 3

Reviewing homework   At the beginning of the session, I check each person's ABC assessment and offer corrective feedback where relevant.

Teaching disputing of ego irrational beliefs   A central task of group members in a self-acceptance group is to learn how to dispute their musturbatory and self-downing irrational beliefs. Thus, I devote the bulk of this session to teaching this core skill. As DiGiuseppe (1991) has shown, disputing involves group members asking themselves three different types of question of their irrational ego beliefs: (a) are they consistent with reality?; (b) are they logical?; (c) do they yield healthy results? As I showed in the first half of this chapter, the answer to these questions is 'no' when they are applied to self-downing beliefs (see Dryden, 1994, for a full discussion of why musturbatory beliefs are also inconsistent with reality, illogical and yield unhealthy results for the individual concerned).

Disputing also involves helping group members to construct preferential and self-accepting beliefs as healthy alternatives to their irrational ego beliefs. So I spend a good deal of the third session helping group members to construct rational ego beliefs.

Homework: identifying and disputing irrational ego beliefs in specific situations   Armed with their new skill of disputing irrational ego beliefs and constructing alternative rational ego beliefs, group members are now ready to put this new skill into practice in their everyday lives before the next session. This forms the basis for the homework assignment for that week.

Session 4

Reviewing homework   I begin by reviewing the previous week's homework assignment and offering corrective feedback as before.

Teaching the rational portfolio method   As mentioned above, disputing irrational beliefs is a core client skill in rational-emotive behaviour therapy in general and in self-acceptance groups in particular. As I have recently shown (Dryden, 1995c), the purpose of disputing in the present context is to help group members understand why their irrational ego beliefs are irrational and why their alternative rational ego beliefs are rational. Once group members have understood this point, they need additional help to enable them to integrate this understanding into their belief system so that it influences for the better the way they think and feel about themselves and the way they act in the world. Helping them to develop a rational portfolio of arguments in favour of their rational ego beliefs and against their irrational ego beliefs is the cognitive technique that I use to initiate this integration process.

Having introduced the idea of the rational portfolio, I suggest that group members spend about 20 minutes in the session developing their own portfolio of arguments. Then I ask them to work in two small groups, reviewing one another's arguments and suggesting additional arguments. During this time I act as consultant, listening to the small group discussion, offering feedback on the arguments developed and being available as a troubleshooter if either of the groups gets stuck.

Homework   For homework I suggest that group members review and add to the arguments they have developed for their rational portfolio. I also suggest that they make a particular note of any arguments about which they have objections, reservations or doubts, or that they do not find persuasive.

Session 5

Reviewing homework   I begin by reviewing the previous week's homework, paying particular attention to arguments about which group members have objections, doubts or reservations or do not find persuasive. I initiate a group discussion on these arguments and intervene to correct misconceptions or to provide additional explanations to help dispel these doubts, etc. and to make their rational arguments more persuasive.

Teaching the zigzag technique   As noted above, it is common for people to respond to their own rational arguments developed in favour of a self-accepting philosophy with what might be called irrational rebuttals i.e. arguments which cast doubt on the concept of self-acceptance and which in fact advocate a return to the philosophy of self-downing. The zigzag technique formalizes this debate between the irrational and rational 'parts' of the person and gives the person practice at defending her rational ego belief against her own irrational attack. This technique helps group members to integrate their rational ego beliefs into their belief system.

In the zigzag technique, the group member begins by writing down a rational ego belief and rating her degree of conviction in this belief on a 0–100 rating scale. Then she responds to this belief with an irrational argument, which she then rebuts. The group member continues in this vein until she has responded to all of her attacks and can think of no more. She then re-rates her degree of conviction in her rational ego belief, which is usually increased if the person used the technique properly.

Once I have taught the group members the rudiments of this technique I ask them to carry out the technique on their own in the session. I stress the importance of keeping to the point, since it is easy for the person to get sidetracked when using this technique. As group members do this task I go from person to person ensuring that they are doing it correctly and, in particular, keep the focus of the debate on their target rational ego belief (see Dryden, 1995c for an extended discussion of the zigzag technique).

Teaching tape-recorded disputing   Tape-recorded disputing is similar to the zigzag method in that group members put the dialogue between their rational and irrational ego beliefs on tape. In addition to emphasizing once again that it is important to keep to the point while using this method, it is useful to stress that group members respond to their irrational attacks with force and energy. It should be explained that since people often hold their irrational ego beliefs very strongly, weak rational responses will have little lasting effect on irrational attacks. It is useful to give the group members some examples so that they can discriminate between weak and forceful disputing (see Dryden, 1995c for an extended discussion of tape-recorded disputing).

Homework   Tape-recorded disputing is a good homework assignment to set at this point, but it is important to establish first that group members all have access to tape recorders. If not, suitable arrangements should be made for them to gain such access. In addition, I usually suggest that group members read and note any objections to Chapter 4 of Paul Hauck's 1991 book, which considers the importance of behavioural methods in the development of self-acceptance. This will be the focus of the next two group sessions.

Session 6

Reviewing homework   In checking group members' tapes, it is important to pay particular attention to their ability to stay focused on the target beliefs and to the tone they used during disputing, and suitable feedback should be given on these two points. As with other reading material, particular emphasis should be given to group members' reservations about the place of behavioural methods in developing self-acceptance.

Providing a rational for the conjoint use of cognitive and behavioural methods in real-life settings   REBT theory states that behavioural methods have a central role to play in the therapeutic change process. Unless group members act on their rational ego beliefs, the benefits they will derive from the group will ultimately be minimal. However, the power of behavioural techniques is best harnessed when they are used conjointly with cognitive methods designed to give group members the opportunity to practise their rational ego beliefs in a real-life setting.

Negotiating behavioural-cognitive tasks   After you have provided group members with a rationale for the conjoint use of behavioural and cognitive techniques, it is important to encourage them by setting one or two behavioural-cognitive tasks which they can implement as homework assignments before the next group session. These tasks should preferably be related to group members' goals.

Teaching rational-emotive imagery   Rational-emotive imagery (REI) is an evocative technique designed to give group members practice in strengthening their rational ego beliefs in the face of negative activating events (As). In self-acceptance groups I suggest the use of REI as preparation for the implementation of the behavioural-cognitive techniques discussed above. Once group members have set a behavioural-cognitive technique, I ask them to imagine a worst-case scenario which constitutes the A in an ABC episode and have them identify and get in touch with an ego-related, disturbed negative emotion (e.g. hurt). Then, while they are still imagining the same negative A, I ask them to change their emotion to a self-accepting, healthy negative emotion. As I have noted elsewhere (Dryden, 1995c), group members achieve this by changing their irrational ego beliefs to rational ego beliefs (see Dryden, 1995c for a fuller discussion of REI).

Homework For homework, I suggest that group members practise REI three times a day for a few days before implementing their behavioural-cognitive tasks.

Session 7

Reviewing homework In checking group members' use of REI, you need to make sure that they did, in fact, change their irrational ego beliefs to their rational alternatives rather than change the negative activating event to something more positive. In reviewing their behavioural-cognitive tasks, you need to ensure that they actually faced the situation that they wanted to confront or acted in the manner planned, and that they practised thinking rationally while doing so.

Agreeing other behavioural-cognitive tasks If members were successful in implementing their behavioural-cognitive assignment it is important to capitalize on this success by negotiating two additional behavioural tasks. Encourage group members to choose tasks that are challenging, but not overwhelming for them. However, if any group member struggled with their initial behavioural-cognitive task, you will have to be less adventurous in the next such assignment you negotiate with that person.

Explaining and agreeing shame-attacking exercises Shame-attacking exercises involve group members acting in a so-called 'shameful' manner and accepting themselves as they do so. They should attract attention to themselves without alarming others, breaking the law or getting themselves into trouble at work. Examples of good shame-attacking exercises are as follows:

- wearing different-coloured shoes;
- asking to see a three-piece suite in a sweet shop;
- singing off-key in public;
- asking for directions to a road one is already in.

I suggest that group members do at least one shame-attacking exercise before the final group session.

Homework The last set of homework assignments is as described above. In addition, I ask group members to come to the last session

---

SELF ACCEPTANCE QUIZ

GIVE REASONS FOR EACH ANSWER

1 Having the love of a significant other makes you a more worthwhile person.
   True or false?

2 If someone you admire is better than you at an important activity, he or she is a better person than you.
   True or false?

3 If you fail at something really important, you are not a failure, but a fallible human being.
   True or false?

4 You can give a human being a single global rating which completely accounts for them.
   True or false?

5 Someone who rapes a small child is wicked through and through.
   True or false?

6 Mother Theresa has more worth than Adolf Hitler.
   True or false?

Figure 9.1 *Self-acceptance quiz*

prepared to talk about what they have achieved from the group and to give feedback about their experience of being in the group.

Session 8

Reviewing homework For the last time, I check on group members' homework assignments and give corrective feedback as usual. Group members are usually keen to learn about one another's shame-attacking exercises and this generates a sense of fun which, in my opinion, is quite suitable to the ending of a group of this educational nature.

The self-acceptance quiz In the spirit of fun and to assess what group members have learned, I ask them to complete in writing a short written quiz (see Figure 9.1).

Why not do the quiz yourself to see what you have learned from this chapter?

Evaluating progress and eliciting feedback on the group I then ask group members to relate what progress they have made towards self-acceptance and whether or not they have achieved their goals. I also ask them to give feedback on the group experience, my way of running it and how it might be improved. Since all group members are involved in other groups in the hospital and many are also in individual psychotherapy, it has not been possible for me to carry out formal research into the effectiveness of self-acceptance groups.

Helping group members to maintain and extend their gains The final task that I ask group members to do is to develop a list of ways of maintaining and extending the gains that they have made from participating in the group (see Dryden, 1995b and 1995c for a fuller discussion of these two points). I stress that they have taken the first few steps along the road to self-acceptance and that how far they go along this road will largely be dependent on the amount of work that they are prepared to do on themselves using the methods that I have taught them during the group. On this point, I wish them well and we say our goodbyes.

References

DiGiuseppe, R. (1991) 'Comprehensive cognitive disputing in RET', in M.E. Bernard (ed.), *Using Rational-Emotive Therapy Effectively*. New York: Plenum Press.

Dryden, W. (1994) *Invitation to Rational-Emotive Psychology*. London: Whurr.

Dryden, W. (1995a) *Preparing for Client Change in Rational Emotive Behaviour Therapy*. London: Whurr.

Dryden, W. (1995b) *Facilitating Client Change in Rational Emotive Behaviour Therapy*. London: Whurr.

Dryden, W. (1995c) *Brief Rational Emotive Behaviour Therapy*. Chichester: Wiley.

Ellis, A. (1972) *Psychotherapy and the Value of a Human Being*. New York: Institute for Rational-Emotive Therapy.

Ellis, A. (1994) *Reason and Emotion in Psychotherapy: A Comprehensive Method of Treating Human Disturbances*, revised and updated edn. New York: Birch Lane Press.

Hauck, P. (1991) *Hold Your Head Up High*. London: Sheldon Press.

Maultsby, M.C. Jr. (1984) *Rational Behavior Therapy*. Englewood Cliffs, NJ: Prentice-Hall.

10

Using REBT in the Supervision of Counsellors

About 15 years ago I discussed some of the advantages of employing audio-tape procedures in counselling and supervision (Dryden,
1981). I pointed out in that article that listening to trainee counsellors' accounts of their counselling sessions and hearing audio
tapes of these sessions often reveals important discrepancies. For
example, in a group supervision session, one trainee told the group
about the interventions she employed with a client experiencing
extreme examination anxiety. She stated that she covered a number
of important concepts with the client. She discussed with him: (1)
the important healing qualities of unconditional self-acceptance; (2)
the mediating effects that cognitions have on emotional experience;
(3) the value of focusing on task-relevant cognitions and editing out
task-irrelevant thoughts in evaluative situations; (4) the benefit of
concentrating on one piece of revision at a time rather than on the
entire revision schedule; and (5) the importance of taking regular
short breaks from study. She indicated that the client understood
these concepts and received great benefit from the discussion.
However, while listening to the tape of the session, it emerged that
the trainee covered all of these points in one long 90-second
statement. Whilst the client claimed to understand these concepts, it
was obvious to all that he was confused. The value of recording
counselling sessions is therefore apparent.

However, trainees often experience anxiety about using cassette
recorders in counselling and supervision and this theme will be
developed in the present chapter.

Manifestations of Trainee Recording and Supervision Anxiety

Supervision of trainees' audio-taped counselling sessions was an
important component of the one-year postgraduate Diploma in
Counselling in Educational Settings' course offered at Aston University (1970–84). Prospective trainees were informed of this and they

This chapter was originally published in W. Dryden, *Dryden on Counselling, Vol. 3: Training and Supervision*. London: Whurr, 1991.

knew that places on the course were contingent upon their agreement to make tapes of actual counselling sessions. In the first term of the course, trainees taped their peer-counselling sessions and thus became quite familiar with being recorded while counselling. They should have thus achieved a fair measure of habituation to making audio tapes of counselling sessions before seeing clients on placement. However, a significant number of trainees initially experienced debilitating anxiety which interfered both with their counselling work and with their ability to learn from supervision. This anxiety generally took several different forms.

SHOWING OVERCONCERN FOR CLIENTS

A number of trainees expressed exaggerated concern for the impact that recording counselling sessions had on clients. They feared that clients would be psychologically damaged if they even raised the topic of tape recording. In my many years' experience of asking clients for permission to record sessions, the vast majority readily agree and, as far as I am aware, none were damaged by my request. My practice is to be thoroughly honest in my request. I point out that it is helpful for me to listen back to sessions and to receive supervision on them. I guarantee that only my supervisor and supervision group will listen to them and that the tapes will be wiped clean afterwards. I tell clients that whilst taping sessions is helpful to me, my primary concern is for their well-being. If they prefer not to have sessions recorded, their wish will be respected and I emphasize the primacy of their decision. When I discussed this with trainees, they were often then able to express their own anxiety underlying their stated concern for clients – anxiety concerning the impact that recording counselling sessions would have on *them*.

'I DON'T HAVE A TAPE THIS WEEK'

In my experience of supervising tapes, I have been impressed with the range of 'reasons' which trainees give either for not making tapes or for not having audible tapes of counselling sessions for supervision. This occurs despite the fact that they receive clear instructions concerning the attainment of clearly audible tape recordings. The 'reasons' I have received can be grouped as follows:

Plug Faults

- The plug did not contain a fuse.
- The plug contained a defective or incorrect fuse.
- The plug wires were not properly attached.

Mains faults

- The mains lead was not attached to the recorder.
- The mains lead was not inserted into the wall socket.
- The socket switch was not turned on.

Microphone Faults

- The external microphone was not attached (or not properly attached) to the recorder;
- Batteries were not inserted into the battery-operated microphone;
- The microphone was placed incorrectly so that clear recording could not be obtained;
- The external microphone was not powerful enough to register voices clearly.

Battery Faults

- Batteries were not inserted into the battery-operated recorder;
- 'Dead' or fading batteries were used (batteries not regularly checked);
- Batteries were incorrectly inserted into the recorder;
- Too few batteries were inserted into the recorder;
- Batteries were left in the recorder, causing corrosion;
- The battery pack had not been recharged;
- The battery pack had been incorrectly inserted into the recorder.

Recording Faults

- Incorrect controls were depressed while 'recording'.
- No controls were depressed while 'recording'.
- A radio programme was recorded instead of the counselling session (when a radio-cassette recorder was used).
- An indistinct recording was made (either because an internal microphone was employed which was not sensitive enough to record clearly or because recording and erasing heads were not regularly cleaned).

Recorder Faults

- The recorder was faulty in 'recording' mode.
- Interference was present on the recording.
- The recorder picked up local police or taxi broadcasts in 'recording' mode which masked the recording of the counselling session.

Tape Faults

- No tape was inserted into the recorder.
- The tape was incorrectly inserted into the recorder.
- The tape was inappropriate for recording purposes.

Trainees who were not particularly anxious about recording counselling sessions generally made clearly audible cassette recordings which they regularly brought to supervision. Thus, it is probable that anxious trainees *tacitly* (i.e. outside their awareness) developed self-defeating ways of defending against their own anxiety. Helping these trainees to acknowledge their anxiety proved difficult, but was best done by encouraging them to explore how they would feel if they had made audible tapes which they would then present for supervision.

TRAINEE BEHAVIOUR IN COUNSELLING SESSIONS

The behaviour that anxious trainees manifested in counselling sessions often provided clues to their recording and supervision anxiety. Such trainees were often 'forgetful'; they 'forgot' to take their recorder (microphone, cassettes or mains lead) to the sessions or they 'forgot' to introduce the topic of recording at the beginning of counselling interviews. When they did remember, they claimed that their clients were 'far too upset' to make clear decisions concerning recording. When they did introduce the topic to clients, they did so hesitantly or ineptly so that their clients refused.

When they did record their sessions they tended to: (1) play safe, by being extremely passive in interviews or by parroting client statements verbatim; (2) talk too much and ask irrelevant questions when silences occurred; (3) display many paraverbal clues to anxiety; and (4) often misunderstand what their clients were trying to express.

TRAINEE BEHAVIOUR IN SUPERVISION

Trainees who were particularly anxious about recording their counselling sessions often displayed typical behaviour patterns in supervision. They often: (1) 'forgot' to bring in tapes for supervision; (2) brought in the 'wrong' tape; (3) tried to engage the supervisor and/or the supervision group in theoretical discussions about the counselling process; (4) opted to present their tapes last hoping for a truncated period of supervision; (5) spent considerable periods of supervision time trying to find the precise segment of tape which they wished to play; (6) tended to deny or distort positive feedback; (7) played segments of counselling sessions which contained plenty of client talk but little counsellor intervention; and (8) played numerous 'games' that have been admirably documented by Kadushin (1968) which were designed to distract supervisors' attention from their actual counselling work.

Understanding Trainee Recording and Supervision Anxiety

It was important in attempting to understand trainees' anxiety about recording counselling sessions to focus on the inferences that they made and the beliefs they held about the recording and supervision process.

INFERENTIAL DISTORTIONS

Inferences are cognitive processes that are either interpretative and/ or evaluative in nature, but do not themselves account for people's emotional experiences. They indicate how people interpret the data that are available to them in their perceptual field. Inferences can of course be accurate or distorted. They are best regarded as hypotheses about the nature of reality and can thus be subjected to empirical enquiry. Unfortunately, anxious trainees often regarded their inferences as facts and thus not amenable to such enquiry. Since anxiety is an emotion that generally involves anticipations of future threat, it is not surprising to find that anxious trainees frequently made a number of distorted inferences concerning the future implications of their present behaviour. Identifying such inferential distortions was done by either examining trainees' *in vivo* automatic thoughts (Beck et al., 1979) or by helping them to articulate the private meanings that the recording and supervision process held for them. Burns (1980) has developed the pioneering work of Aaron Beck (compare Beck et al., 1979) on the common forms of inferential distortions that depressed and anxious clients typically make. Burns's 'types of twisted thinking' will be used as a framework for presenting the most common inferential errors that anxious trainees make concerning the personal implications of the recording and supervision process.

All-or-nothing Thinking

Here trainees typically employed black-or-white categories to process information. All-or-nothing thinking commonly leads to perfectionism and feelings of failure. Thus, one trainee reported observing herself making an inaccurate summary of her client's concerns and concluded: 'I've ruined this interview completely.'

Overgeneralization

Anxious trainees often saw a single event as a perpetual pattern of defeat. Words like 'always' and 'never' are clues that overgeneralizations were being made. Such trainees often become easily discouraged and hopeless about their ability to learn and internalize constructive counselling skills. One trainee reported thinking that if he did not master the technique of systematic desensitization quickly, then he would never learn it.

Mental Filter

Commonly, anxious trainees focused on a single negative detail and dwelt on it obsessively so that their ability to make objective perceptions of reality became impaired. One trainee became so anxious about gaining her clients' approval that she habitually gave them extra time instead of terminating sessions punctually. She reported having the thought that, if one of her clients showed disapproval, then she would continually focus on this, thus editing out the total picture which indicated that many of her clients were benefiting quite well from their counselling sessions with her.

Disqualifying the Positive

Anxious trainees tended to reject positive experiences when they occurred by saying that they didn't count. Such processes frequently occurred in supervision groups. For example, one trainee consistently denied that he was doing well with a socially anxious client (he was in fact helping her quite considerably), insisting that it was such an easy case (which it wasn't) that anybody would have been successful.

Jumping to Conclusions

Anxious trainees often acted as if they had extrasensory perception. They consistently interpreted events in a negative manner in the absence of corroborating evidence. There are two major types of 'conclusion-jumping': mind-reading and negative prediction.

Mind-reading Here anxious trainees predicted that their clients would have negative thoughts about them, the counselling process and the issue of tape recording. They regarded such inferences as 'facts' as opposed to 'hypotheses' and thus rarely attempted to test their validity. For example, one trainee came to supervision in a distressed state because she was certain that one of her clients had not kept an appointment because he regarded her as a 'useless novice'. It transpired that the client had been involved in a minor traffic accident, had tried to contact the counselling service by telephone to cancel his appointment but could not get through. In counselling, practitioners are not commonly in a position to ascertain reasons for client non-attendance and dropout. Consequently, such ambiguity contributes to the perpetuation of self-defeating mind-reading.

Negative prediction   Anxious trainees often anticipated that counselling sessions would turn out badly and thus they frequently predicted disasters. One trainee predicted that he would fail to understand his new overseas client, and got into an anxious state which severely interfered with his ability to listen and empathize with the client. As can be seen, negative predictions often become self-fulfilling prophecies.

Magnification and/or Minimization

In magnification, anxious trainees exaggerated the importance of their difficulties in learning and internalizing counselling skills. They 'forgot' that most people would be uncomfortable learning new techniques and methods and regarded their discomfort in a very negative light. In minimization, trainees undervalued their own skills and talents while praising their fellow trainees for these very same skills and talents.

Emotional Reasoning

This occurs when people assume that their feelings constitute evidence as to the nature of reality. Thus, anxious trainees concluded that their anxiety was valid proof of their inadequacy as counsellors. One trainee argued that taping counselling sessions was dangerous because he felt anxious about it.

Labelling

This is an extreme form of overgeneralization. Instead of acknowledging that they merely made errors or poorly executed counselling interventions, anxious trainees were much more likely to conclude that they were 'inadequate counsellors' than were less anxious trainees. The latter were more likely to acknowledge their errors in skill and technique without placing a pejorative label on their ability as counsellors.

Personalization

Here anxious trainees were prone to assume almost total responsibility for the counselling process when it was going badly and virtually no responsibility when it was going well. They tended to be constantly looking for evidence that their clients were dissatisfied with their services. This vigilance perpetuated their anxiety, which consequently impeded their learning. Trainees who were to be seen frequently checking for the arrival of unpunctual clients often made such personalizing inferences.

PERSONAL WORTH AND FATE CONTROL

The analysis presented above provides a helpful way of classifying the inferential distortions made by trainees anxious about recording and presenting their counselling interviews for supervision. Most frequently, trainees' inferential distortions reflect concerns about either *personal worth* or *fate control*. It is important to note that the same inferential distortions may reflect these very different underlying concerns. For example, consider Jack and Sylvia, two counselling trainees who were both anxious in case what they considered to be poor examples of counselling technique would incur the disapproval of their respective supervisors. Both predicted that such disapproval was virtually certain to occur. However, while Jack was anxious because he was basing his personal worth on his supervisor's anticipated response, Sylvia was anxious that her supervisor's disapproval would influence him to give her poor job references which would, in her mind, ruin her career in counselling before it had commenced. Sylvia thus viewed her supervisor as having enormous control over her fate, whilst Jack viewed his supervisor as having enormous control over his personal worth.

Trainees who experienced 'personal worth' anxiety tended to predict that their errors (which they inevitably made in learning how to counsel) would lead their supervisors and fellow trainees to make negative judgements, not only of their counselling ability but also of their personal worth. They thus implicitly construed other people as harsh critics, intolerant of human fallibility. This (as will be shown later) was really a projection of their own intolerant attitude towards themselves. They were really harsh critics of themselves. However, trainees with 'fate control' anxiety predicted that their supervisors would note their errors and use this information against them in ways that would adversely affect their future aspirations (e.g. by giving them failing grades or writing them poor references). They did not consider that their supervisors viewed such errors as an inevitable part of learning new skills. They thus construed their supervisors as malevolent individuals who would not make allowances for the fundamental processes of human learning. Again, as will be shown later, this view was generally a projection of their own attitude towards themselves and the world. They believed that they must not make errors and, when they did, they would consequently be punished. They sometimes did fail to gain their counselling qualification, but this was to a large extent a self-fulfilling prophecy because their 'fate control' anxiety seriously impaired their ability to learn from the feedback that they were given.

IRRATIONAL BELIEFS

It is a fundamental assumption of REBT that inferential distortions stem from people's irrational beliefs (A. Ellis, personal communication). Irrational beliefs are evaluations of personal significance couched in devout, dogmatic and absolute terms. They reflect a philosophy of demandingness and are stated as 'musts', 'shoulds', 'oughts' and 'have-tos' and generally account for people's emotional experiences.

Dryden (1984) has argued that there are two fundamental human disturbances – *ego disturbance* and *discomfort disturbance* – which of course take a myriad of different forms. Trainees who experienced 'personal worth' anxiety were clearly exemplifying ego disturbance. They profoundly believed the idea 'that you can give yourself a global rating as a human and that your general worth and self-acceptance depends on the goodness of your performances and the degree that people approve of you' (Ellis, 1977a). They tended to make global ratings of their 'selves' which were conditional on (1) their counselling abilities; (2) the extent to which their clients improved; and (3) the feedback they received from their supervisors and, to a lesser extent, their fellow trainees. They overgeneralized from rating their present performance as trainee counsellors to rating their full potential ability as counsellors and thence made global ratings of their 'selves'. If they could articulate their underlying philosophy it would be thus: 'Because I am not doing very well at the moment in my counselling, I will never do well and therefore will always be an ineffective counsellor which will prove that I am worthless.' The statement: 'I am worthless' is derived from the premise: 'I must do well and be approved.' Believing this, they remained anxious even when they performed well, because they further believed that they *must* maintain that good performance in the future. These irrational beliefs underpin the inferential distortions that this group of anxious trainees made concerning the reactions of their clients, supervisors and fellow trainees. Since they were harsh critics of themselves, they once again predicted that others would make similarly harsh judgements of them.

Trainees who had discomfort disturbance wanted to enter the counselling profession, but escalated their desires into absolute demands. Their underlying philosophy was: 'I must get what I want at all costs.' If they did not get what they believed they must, they concluded that *it was awful* and that they *could not stand* being deprived. Since they regarded getting what they wanted as absolutely necessary, they tended to be extremely sensitive to perceived threats to goal attainment. This underlying belief then accounted for their inferential distortions, since even constructive negative feedback constituted a severe threat to what they believed they must have. Other people, and particularly their supervisors, were thus seen as malevolent individuals who would deprive them of their sacred goals and, consequently, were viewed as having enormous control over their fate. These trainees did not necessarily attach their personal worth to the attainment of their goals, although some may also have done this. Trainees with 'pure' discomfort disturbance believed that they must get what they wanted merely because they desired it, whilst other trainees with ego disturbance believed that they must get what they wanted in order to prove to themselves that they were worthwhile individuals.

As Dryden, Trower and Casey (1983) have shown, ego disturbance and discomfort disturbance are often interacting processes. Thus, one trainee who believed that she must do well in counselling interviews (ego disturbance) became anxious. This anxiety activated her belief that she could not stand feeling anxious (discomfort disturbance), which in turn triggered her further belief that such heightened anxiety proved her worthlessness (ego disturbance). Indeed many trainees trapped themselves in the interlocking web of their ego and discomfort-related beliefs.

In this section, trainee anxiety about the recording and supervision process has been considered. The manifestations of this anxiety were detailed and a framework for understanding its determinants was outlined. The emphasis of the following section will be on how supervisors can help trainees overcome the debilitating effects of recording and supervision anxiety so that they can maximise their learning.

Overcoming Obstacles to Trainee Learning: Fostering a Helpful Climate in Supervision

It is important to realize that whilst not all trainees will be anxious about presenting audio tapes of their counselling sessions for supervision, virtually all will be apprehensive. As a supervisor I have found that applying the following principles is most beneficial in fostering a helpful climate in both individual and group supervision sessions. The promotion of a helpful climate is highly desirable if anxious trainees are to be encouraged to acknowledge and deal with their anxieties.

UNCONDITIONAL ACCEPTANCE

It is beneficial if supervisors show that they can unconditionally accept their trainees as fallible human beings. This means that whilst supervisors may rate certain aspects, behaviours or skills which their trainees may display, they endeavour not to rate the 'personhood' of trainees (Ellis, 1972). For example, I once had occasion to reproach one of my trainees for consistent unpunctuality at counselling sessions.

> Look, frankly I consider your behaviour in this regard to be pretty bad. We've discovered some of the reasons for it and though you claim to understand why you do it, you keep doing it. However, I want you to know that while I dislike your behaviour, I really don't feel badly at all about you as a total complex ever-changing person. While I think your behaviour stinks, you're not a stinker. And of course we've discovered that you have a lot of assets in your counselling. Now the reality is that counsellors who aren't punctual . . .

The trainee in question appreciated the honest expression of my annoyance concerning her behaviour and realized that I was not either in tone or words damning her as a person.

Supervisors would be wise to dispute their own internal intolerant demands about the behaviour of their trainees and replace these with their honest un-devout preferences. In this way they will be able effectively to communicate unconditional acceptance of trainees, whilst honestly expressing their positive and negative reactions to trainee behaviour, when appropriate.

SUPERVISOR SELF-DISCLOSURE

Anxious trainees often view their supervisors as infallible and fantasize that such superhuman beings learned how to counsel effortlessly and without error. It is important for supervisors to refuse to be seduced into this fantasy and openly acknowledge their past and present counselling errors. This serves to help trainees learn that: (1) errors are an inevitable part of becoming skilled counsellors; (2) counsellors do not suddenly stop making errors after completion of training; (3) it is possible to acknowledge errors openly without defensiveness and self-blame; and (4) supervisors who are tolerant of their own errors are likely to be tolerant of trainees' errors.

EXPLAINING THE NATURE OF HUMAN LEARNING

It is often helpful if supervisors discuss the nature of human learning with trainees at an early stage in the supervision process. It is important to stress that making errors is a natural and inevitable stage of learning any new set of complex skills – including counselling. In fact, I have found it useful to introduce a note of levity into this discussion. I usually add that any trainee who does not make errors will be ceremoniously thrown out of the supervision group. I also challenge and overthrow the myth that trainee counsellors will seriously damage clients by their errors – adding of course that this group will be the exception and I shall thus order several ambulances to stand by to ferry quivering clients to the nearest sanctuary called 'The Dryden home for clients damaged by trainees'. I, of course, stress that there is usually a long waiting list!

THE JUDICIOUS USE OF HUMOUR

I sometimes judiciously use humour in running supervision groups in a similar manner to its use in counselling. I do so because basically I agree with Ellis (1977b), who argues that one way of viewing emotional disturbance is that it stems from people taking themselves, others and the world *too* seriously. Anxious trainees definitely take themselves, the counselling role and the counselling process *too* seriously. I have found it highly therapeutic to challenge this viewpoint directly and indirectly with humour. I am often the butt of my own jokes (it is helpful to introduce humour into supervision in this way) and show in this manner that I do not take myself *too* seriously both in and out of counselling sessions. I show that I can laugh at some of the stupid things I have done while taking a compassionate and accepting attitude towards myself. The therapeutic use of humour with trainees had better be done within a spirit of unconditional acceptance. My intention is to direct my humorous comments to what trainees *do* and never at who they *are*. It is important for supervisors to elicit feedback from trainees concerning the impact of humorous interventions. Not all trainees appreciate it and find it helpful!

GIVING BALANCED FEEDBACK

I have found that trainees benefit most from receiving *both* positive *and* constructive negative feedback from their supervisors concerning their counselling work. Supervisors who consistently focus on trainees' errors unwittingly reinforce the self-defeating attitudes of trainees with 'personal worth' and 'fate control' anxieties. The receipt of consistent negative feedback encourages trainees with 'personal worth' anxiety to blame themselves for their errors and those with 'fate control' anxiety to think that their future aspirations are being seriously threatened, since the supervisor concerned will surely give them failing grades. However, receiving consistent positive feedback does not encourage either group of trainees to believe that they are learning very much about counselling. Whilst such feedback may not directly evoke their respective anxieties, it does lead to a different kind of anxiety. Such trainees are reasonably sure that they are making counselling errors but are never told what these are. They either become anxious about this uncertainty or anxious about their own inability to determine their errors for themselves.

I thus strive to provide a balance between positive and constructive negative feedback given in a spirit of unconditional acceptance of trainees as people. I even reinforce this with humour by saying to trainees with 'personal worth' anxiety: (1) 'That was a good response, but it doesn't make you a great person' and (2) 'That wasn't a very good response, but it doesn't make you a rotten person.' To trainees with 'fate control' anxiety I may say: (1) 'That wasn't a particularly good response, but we won't throw you out just yet', and (2) 'That was a good response, we'll definitely throw you out if you keep that standard up.'

Parenthetically, when giving trainees either positive or constructive negative feedback, it is best to make such feedback as *concrete* as possible. Vague feedback does not encourage trainees to identify what they are doing right or wrong, and in the latter case they are not helped to consider specific alternatives.

EXPLAINING 'PERSONAL WORTH' AND 'FATE CONTROL' ANXIETIES

It is beneficial to explain to trainees at an early stage the nature of 'personal worth' and 'fate control' anxieties and to point out that these are both common, albeit dysfunctional, experiences. Providing such explanations makes it easier for trainees honestly to admit to these fears and it thus undercuts trainee defensiveness. This is particularly so when trainees can see that others in the group share similar anxieties. It is this factor of 'universality' that helps the supervision group become a therapeutic milieu for its members (Yalom, 1975). When trainees see that they are not alone in experiencing anxiety about the recording and supervision process, they tend to feel less shameful of these fears and thus become less defensive about their experiences.

Overcoming Obstacles to Trainee Learning: Dealing with Trainee Anxiety in Supervision

Whilst it is important to delineate boundaries between supervision and personal therapy, I find that the two processes sometimes necessarily overlap. When the factors described in the previous section do not fully allay trainees' fears, it is beneficial if supervisors help trainees to identify and deal with their anxieties if the latter are to maximize their learning from the supervisory experience. However, these therapeutic encounters are generally restricted to an exploration of trainees' anxieties about recording and supervision, and supervisors had better not deal with trainees' other personal problems in the supervision group since this tends to lead to difficult role-conflict problems. When I attempt to deal with trainees' recording- and supervision-related anxieties in supervision groups, I find it best first to seek permission to do this. I explain to the trainee in question that we could deal with the issue here in the group setting or, if the trainee prefers, the issue could be dealt with outside in personal therapy with someone else. If permission is not sought and granted, trainees may understandably become defensive during the ensuing discussion. Once permission is granted, my role is then to help trainees identify, challenge and change the inferential distortions and the irrational beliefs that underlie their anxieties and negative inferences.

The following segments represent two examples of how to deal with trainees' anxieties about recording and supervision in the context of supervision groups.

DEALING WITH 'PERSONAL WORTH' ANXIETY

Stephanie, the trainee in question, had on several occasions failed to bring audio tapes of her counselling sessions to the group for supervision.

> *Supervisor*: OK Stephanie, I would like to say something here. My guess is that you may have some anxiety about making tapes or presenting them for supervision here and this issue needs addressing in some context. What do you think?
> *Trainee*: Well . . . I guess you are right . . . I know I don't like making tapes. It does seem to be valuable . . . for other people. I guess I'm anxious about it. It certainly is on my mind a lot.
> *Supervisor*: OK, look. We can either discuss it here and now or if you

wish you can discuss it with someone else . . . I mean . . . with someone else not concerned with your evaluation. [*The supervisor gives the trainee a 'choice' to deal with the issue in the group or elsewhere. He seeks 'permission' to discuss it further.*]

Trainee: Well . . . since we're here, why don't we do it now?

Supervisor: All right. Now would you agree with my hunch that you're anxious?

Trainee: Yes, that's right.

Supervisor: What are you anxious about specifically?

Trainee: Well . . . if I knew no one would listen to my tapes, I wouldn't mind recording my interviews. It's just . . . the thought of . . . well . . . you all hearing my counselling.

Supervisor: So you're anxious about the group listening to you on tape. What's scary about that?

Trainee: Oh God! . . . well . . . it's the . . . thought I guess about what you all . . . no perhaps more about what you specifically are going to think of me.

Supervisor: Right. You're scared that I'm going to think you're a great woman and a scholar. Is that correct? [*General laughter. The supervisor uses humour to loosen the trainee up a little.*]

Trainee: Well hardly. I guess I'm scared . . . that . . . you would think badly of me [*laughs*] if I presented a lousy tape.

Supervisor: But let's assume that. Let's suppose you played a lousy tape, what sort of things do you think I would think of you? [*The supervisor checks out the nature of the trainee's inferences.*]

Trainee: Well . . . [*pause*] . . . the thing that comes to mind is that . . . well the word idiot comes to mind.

Supervisor: So you're scared that you'd present a tape and I'd think what an idiot you were for doing a lousy job? Is that it?

Trainee: Yes.

Supervisor: Now let's assume that I actually do think you're an idiot. Do you also get the sense that I would act on that thought in some way? [*The supervisor seeks to go deeper into the trainee's inference structure. He wishes to assess what type of anxiety – 'personal worth' or 'fate control' – he is dealing with.*]

Trainee: I'm not sure . . . what do you mean?

Supervisor: Well, for example, do you think that I might shout at you and say something like: 'Stephanie you're an idiot', or do you think I'd fail you, or . . .?

Trainee: Oh, I see . . . No, I don't think you would shout at me. I don't think you'd fail me either. It's just . . . I guess that your opinion is pretty important to me. [*The trainee provides clues that it is 'personal worth' rather than 'fate control' anxiety that she is experiencing.*]

Supervisor: Pretty important in what sense?

Trainee: Mmm. . . . That I need you to think well of me.

Supervisor: And if I don't?

Trainee: Then I'd feel pretty lousy.

Supervisor: Could you zero in on that feeling a little more and let me know what kind of lousy feeling it would be?

Trainee: I'd feel depressed.

Supervisor: What would you dwell on in that depressed lousy feeling?

Trainee: On . . . what a failure I am.

Supervisor: So if I understand you. You would play a lousy tape. I would think you were an idiot, you would define yourself as a failure and feel lousy. Is that how it would go?

Trainee: Yes, that's it.

Supervisor: OK. Now as I see it, whether I think you are an idiot is important but not the real issue. You probably need to check it out, however, at some point. Can you see though the link between that definition 'I am a failure' and that lousy depressed feeling? [*The supervisor focuses the trainee on her irrational belief, while indicating also the importance of testing inferences.*]

Trainee: Yes I see it. It's what you said in your lecture on REBT, isn't it?

Supervisor: Right. Now what I also said in that lecture is the importance of checking out whether that belief holds water. As Ellis might say, we want evidence that you would be a failure if you fail to impress me or fail to give a good performance.

Trainee: Well there isn't any. I guess I'd be what you called a fallible human being who is failing to do well at the moment.

Supervisor: That's correct, but look at how hesitantly you said that. You acknowledge it but don't really believe it.

Trainee: Exactly.

Supervisor: How do you think you could really work on believing it?

Trainee: By going over it as you said in the lecture.

Supervisor: Right. Really show yourself that (1) you don't need my approval and (2) if you were a failure you would do what?

Trainee: Fail continually.

Supervisor: At everything? Now if you really worked on that, would you feel anxious about my defining you in my own head as an idiot?

Trainee: No, but I still wouldn't like it.

Supervisor: Quite.

Trainee: But I wouldn't be anxious.

Supervisor: OK. Now if you really believed that, would you then be so sure of what I would be thinking of you?

Trainee: Let me see . . . No . . . I would still have doubts, though.

Supervisor: Right. How could you check out your hunch about what I was thinking?

Trainee: By asking you?

Supervisor: No, by consulting the tea leaves. [*General laughter*]

Trainee: OK! OK! I get your point. [*laughs*]

Supervisor: Why don't you do that work and let us know how you get on next week. OK?

Trainee: OK.

Stephanie really worked on her 'personal worth' anxiety, started to accept herself unconditionally and began to bring in tapes regularly for supervision and did very well in her final assessment.

DEALING WITH 'FATE CONTROL' ANXIETY

Ralph, another trainee, did bring in his audio tapes for supervision, but wasted an inordinate amount of time by discussing theoretical points, by trying to find the exact segment of tape he wished the group to hear and by extending other trainees' supervision time, so that his counselling work wasn't heard.

Supervisor: Well, Ralph. You seem to be doing it again. We're interested in hearing your counselling, not your excellent grasp of theory. Listen. Let me honestly ask you. Why are you so reluctant to play your tapes in here? You say you're not, but your behaviour belies your words.

Trainee: I'm not reluctant.

Supervisor: Let me put it another way. Close your eyes a moment. Really picture this scene. We are going to devote the whole three-hour session to listening to your tapes and we won't allow you to interrupt or anything. . . . Now really picture that scene. How do you honestly feel? [*The supervisor uses the imagery modality to bypass the trainee's tendency to deny feelings: Lazarus, 1978.*]

Trainee: Quite uncomfortable.

Supervisor: OK. Now I'd like to explore that feeling more so that I can help you participate more in the group and play your tapes, but I don't want to force you. Would you like to explore this discomfort here and now? [*The supervisor asks for permission to explore the issue further.*]

Trainee: OK. [*The trainee is hesitant, but the supervisor decides to go along with his stated agreement.*]

Supervisor: Now what would you be uncomfortable about?

Trainee: About you lot listening to my tapes.

Supervisor: If you really focus on that discomfort, what kind of feeling would it be?

Trainee: . . . A mixture of anger and anxiety.

Supervisor: Anxiety about what?

Trainee: Being evaluated.

Supervisor: By whom?

Trainee: Mmmh . . . mainly you. Yes by you.

Supervisor: And the anger?

Trainee: Towards you for making me do it.

Supervisor: OK. Let's go back to your anxiety. What kind of evaluation would you be afraid of getting?

Trainee: A bad one.

Supervisor: OK. Now let's assume, and I want to stress that we're assuming now, let's assume that I do listen to your tapes and give you a bad evaluation. What would be scary about that?

Trainee: I'd be scared that I wouldn't get my counselling diploma.

Supervisor: Let's assume that for the moment. If you don't get your diploma what would that mean? [*The supervisor is aiming to 'chain' the trainee's inferences to get at his core irrational belief.*]

Trainee: That would be awful.

Supervisor: Why is that?

Trainee: Counselling is really what I want to do. I've set my heart on it.

Supervisor: But let's say you were barred for ever from your first choice, what then?

Trainee: . . . well . . . I don't know . . . I'd hate it. It's just a feeling that . . . I just have to get . . . my first choice. [*The trainee reveals in halting fashion his discomfort disturbance.*]

Supervisor: OK. So you start by saying that counselling is really important to you and then you jump, if I understand you correctly, to you *have* to do it. Am I hearing you accurately?

Trainee: Yes.

Supervisor: So your belief is: 'Because it's important to me, I have to get it' or to put it another way, 'I have to get what I want.'

Trainee: That's right.

Supervisor: And then I guess, in your mind, I'm the obstacle.

Trainee: Right. It's funny, that's why I get angry with you. I often see you as kind of in control of . . . my future, almost. [*The trainee clearly reveals his 'fate control' anxiety.*]

Supervisor: Is there any feeling at all, that if you don't get to be a counsellor that you'd be less worthy or anything like that? [*The supervisor is testing to see whether 'personal worth' anxiety is involved in the trainee's concerns.*]

Trainee: No. It's much more the feeling of being deprived of what I want. I'd really hate that.

The supervisor then helped Ralph over subsequent weeks to acknowledge his desire to enter the counselling profession, but to dispute the belief that he *had to* get what he wanted. Ralph was further helped to imagine his future without counselling and eventually began to see that he could be happy in his second or third career choice, although not as happy as he would be working as a counsellor. This helped him to view his supervisor as less of a threat, although some direct interventions were still necessary to help him correct some of his inferential 'fate control' distortions. He passed the course with average grades.

While I have chosen to present examples where trainees revealed 'personal worth' and 'fate control' anxieties in their pure form, in reality much trainee anxiety is a subtle blend of the two. Furthermore, whilst I have detailed two interviews where the entire dialogue occurred between the trainee in question and myself as supervisor, commonly other group members participate in this process as well. In conclusion, the overall aim of supervisors, on their own or with other group members, is to help anxious trainees: (1) acknowledge their anxiety; (2) identify and challenge the inferential distortions and irrational beliefs which underlie their anxiety; and (3) replace these with more accurate inferences and rational beliefs. When this is done successfully, trainees normally become less anxious, regularly present their audio tapes for supervision in a non-defensive manner and generally benefit greatly from supervisory feedback.

References

Beck, A.T., Rush, A.J., Shaw, B.F. and Emery, G. (1979) *Cognitive Therapy of Depression*. New York: Guilford Press.

Burns, D.D. (1980) *Feeling Good: The New Mood Therapy*. New York: William Morrow.

Dryden, W. (1981) 'Some uses of audio-tape procedures in counselling: a personal view', *Counselling*, 36(April): 14–17.

Dryden, W. (1984) 'Rational-emotive therapy (RET)', in W. Dryden (ed.), *Individual Therapy in Britain*. London: Harper and Row.

Dryden, W., Trower, P. and Casey, A. (1983) 'A comprehensive approach to social skills training II: contributions from rational-emotive therapy', *The Counsellor*, 3(7): 2–12.

Ellis, A. (1972) 'Psychotherapy and the value of a human being', in W. Davis (ed.), *Value and Valuation: Aetiological Studies in Honor of Robert A. Hartman*. Knoxville: University of Tennessee Press.

Ellis, A. (1977a) 'Irrational ideas', in J.L. Wolfe and E. Brand (eds), *Twenty Years of Rational Therapy*. New York: Institute for Rational Living.

Ellis, A. (1977b) 'Fun as psychotherapy', *Rational Living*, 12: 2–9.

Kadushin, A. (1968) 'Games people play in supervision', *Social Work*, 13: 23–32.

Lazarus, A. (1978) *In the Mind's Eye*. New York: Rawson.

Yalom, I.D. (1975) *The Theory and Practice of Group Psychotherapy*, 2nd edn. New York: Basic Books.

11

Audio-tape Supervision by Mail: An REBT Perspective

The aims of this chapter are: (1) to describe my approach to supervising by mail the audio-taped counselling sessions of trainee rational emotive behaviour therapists and (2) to discuss some of the issues that arise from this mode of supervision.

The REBT theory of emotions posits that emotional experience is based on evaluative thinking. Two major types of such thinking are identified: rational and irrational. Rational evaluations refer to appraisals of liking or disliking which are stated as personal preferences. Irrational evaluations occur when these personal preferences are escalated to unqualified, absolute demands. Such demands can be made on ourselves, other people and the world. When people rationally desire or prefer something, they further conclude that if they don't get it: (1) it is really inconvenient but not the end of the world; and (2) they are fallible humans with failings and inadequacies, but not worthless, damnable individuals. Consequent to holding this rational belief, they will feel frustrated, concerned, sad or sorry – emotions which are self-enhancing because they are likely to motivate the individuals to try and change the situation or help them to adjust if change is not possible. However, when people change their preferences to demands, namely that since they want something, they absolutely must get it, they will further conclude: (1) it is awful if they don't get it and (2) they are worthless or bad people for failing. Consequent to holding this irrational belief, they are likely to experience anxiety, depression, shame and guilt – emotions which are self-defeating in that they generally impede people from changing the situation or adapting, if change is not possible. REBT theory further posits that individuals can take an almost limitless range of desires, e.g. for love, approval, comfort, control, competence and clarity, and change these to absolute demands. Furthermore, dysfunctional behavioural patterns are deemed to stem from those irrational beliefs.

This chapter was originally published in the *British Journal of Cognitive Psychotherapy*, 1983, 1(1): 57–64.

The major tasks of the REBT therapist are:

(1) to help the patient to share his [the therapist's] theoretical stance that the patient's disturbance has attitudinal antecedents,

(2) to help the patient see that changes in belief will promote emotional and behavioural well-being and

(3) to help the patient acknowledge that he had better continually work at changing his irrational beliefs by cognitive, imaginal and behavioural disputations. (Dryden, 1982: 17)

The major tasks of REBT supervisors, whether they are supervising trainee counsellors in person or by mail, are: (1) to give them feedback on their understanding of the fundamentals of rational-emotive theory as this is manifested in clinical interventions; and (2) to give them feedback on more general clinical skills (Wessler and Ellis, 1980). This dual purpose is implicit in the work of REBT supervisors no matter what training programme trainee counsellors are undertaking.

Most of my supervision work of trainee REBT therapists occurs with those who are undergoing the associate fellowship training scheme which is sponsored by the Institute of Rational-Emotive Therapy in New York. In order to qualify for this programme, trainee counsellors must: (1) have participated in a five-day primary certificate programme in the fundamentals of REBT and (2) hold a recognized counselling, psychology or psychotherapy qualification in the country in which they are employed. To gain associate fellow status, candidates have to (1) participate in two five-day workshops where various topics in advanced rational-emotive theory and practice are covered; and (2) submit 25 of their counselling tapes for supervision. Furthermore their supervisors must testify as to their competence. Candidates are strongly encouraged to submit their tapes to no less than three supervisors, although this regulation may be waived in countries which do not have many accredited supervisors, such as Britain. My experience in supervising trainee counsellors has been almost exclusively limited to supervision of tapes by mail. I have supervised counsellors from London, Dublin, Bristol, Sheffield, Nova Scotia in Canada and various cities in America. The working alliance between myself and trainee counsellors in these programmes is founded on the assumption that I will be giving them feedback on their tapes from an REBT perspective. I encourage supervisees to send me, according to their opinion, both good and bad examples of their work. Occasionally, supervisees only select tapes from counselling sessions that are going well. In this event, I usually confront such supervisees, asking them to reflect on the possible underlying motivations for such behaviour: the need for approval, the need to be seen as competent, etc.

Whether I am supervising trainees in person or by mail, I believe that listening to audio tapes of counselling sessions is paramount to the process of supervision, especially in REBT. Listening to tapes allows me to hear what trainee counsellors say, how they say it, when they say it and if they say it (Garcia, 1976). In my experience, trainee counsellors' accounts of counselling sessions are also important for supervisors to elicit, but on their own do not provide adequate information concerning what actually transpired in the sessions. Obviously video tapes of counselling sessions would provide the non-verbal channel missing from audio tapes. However, such technology is expensive and tape compatibility problems which exist mean that video-tape supervision by mail is not feasible.

The obvious disadvantage of supervising audio-taped counselling sessions by mail is that the immediate dialogue which face-to-face supervision provides is missing. I find that whilst I endeavour to ask supervisees questions while taping my supervisory comments, I experience a tendency to give my own opinions about the counselling session more frequently than I would in face-to-face supervision. On this point, I agree with Garcia (1976) who has said: 'It seems to me that you are a good supervisor not by the answers you give but by the questions you ask.'

Another major disadvantage of supervision by mail is that there is an inevitable delay between trainees conducting counselling sessions and receiving supervision on them. I endeavour to supervise tapes on the day I receive them or no later than the day after receipt. However, it is still doubtful that supervisees will receive my supervision before seeing their clients again.

However, there are advantages to supervising audio tapes by mail. First, it enables trainees to receive comments on their work where distance precludes face-to-face supervision. It is unrealistic to expect one of my supervisees from Dublin, for example, to fly over for a one-hour supervision session, there being no REBT supervisors in Dublin. Secondly, it enables trainees to get feedback from a supervisor with a good reputation where distance is again a problem. If I was limited to face-to-face supervision I would not have been supervised by Albert Ellis as part of my own training programme. Thirdly, this form of supervision allows supervisors to conduct supervision at times convenient to them: I prefer to supervise tapes late at night at a time when I feel most creative.

There are three major ways of supervising audio tapes by mail. Supervisors can: (1) listen to an entire session and then either write or tape their comments; (2) give ongoing written or taped comments while listening to the session; and (3) listen to the entire session first, give general comments and then listen to the session again giving ongoing supervision. My own preference is to tape my comments and provide whatever type of supervision my supervisees find most helpful and can financially afford.

Since I am supervising tapes by mail, I find it even more important to involve my trainees in the supervisory process as much as I can. More specifically I encourage them to formulate their own goals for supervision. I thus ask them at the beginning of our supervisory relationship what they would like to achieve from my supervision and, more specifically, I encourage them to address themselves to concrete concerns about a particular counselling session. I ask them to specify what strengths they demonstrated in the counselling session and how, in retrospect, they would have conducted the session differently. I prefer my supervisees to send me several tapes from a particular ongoing counselling case rather than to send me isolated tapes from several cases. This helps me to hear how my trainees conduct counselling over time and allows me to address this issue in my supervisory feedback. My overall strategy, then, is to stimulate my supervisees' thinking so that they can learn in time to supervise themselves. However, I do believe that it is important for even experienced counsellors to remain in supervision throughout their career. Thus, I had a 10-year co-supervisory relationship with a colleague in Chicago with whom I regularly exchanged tapes for supervision and I periodically send tapes to Albert Ellis for his supervisory comment.

Therapeutic Alliance: A Framework for Supervision

The framework I use for supervising trainee rational-emotive counsellors is one based on recent theorizing on the three dimensions of the therapeutic alliance (Dryden, 1982). From this viewpoint, effective counselling of whatever orientation occurs when: (1) the counsellor and client have a good working interpersonal relationship (the *bond* dimension); (2) both counsellor and client are working together towards helping the client realize his or her goals (the *goal* dimension); and (3) both counsellor and client acknowledge their respective tasks and believe that such tasks are sufficient for the client to reach such goals (the *task* dimension).

FEEDBACK ON THERAPEUTIC 'BONDS'

In giving my supervisees feedback on the quality of the therapeutic bond between them and their clients, I initially address myself to the core therapeutic conditions described by Rogers (1957). First, I pay attention to *counsellor empathy*. I listen in particular to: (1) whether my supervisees encourage their clients to state fully their problems as they see them; (2) whether and how accurately they communicate such understanding, i.e. do they work from their clients' data or do they allow rational-emotive theory to distort such data inappropriately? I also listen closely to the extent to which they *accept* their clients as fallible human beings – are there any signs that they adopt a judgemental attitude towards their clients? I listen for signs that they are not being *genuine* in their encounters with their clients – are they inappropriately adopting a façade?

It is important to realize that Rogers's (1957) original hypothesis stated that the important mechanism for change was the extent to which such counsellor-offered conditions are perceived by clients rather than by external observers (in this case supervisors). Nevertheless, if supervisors put themselves in a particular client's frame of reference, such feedback may have increased reliability. I not only give my supervisees feedback on these attitudes but also ask them to reflect on what intrapsychic obstacles might exist in them that could block the therapeutic expression of such attitudes. Here, as elsewhere on similar matters, the supervisees are left to do such reflection on their own (or perhaps with their own counsellors!)

I then address myself to the extent to which supervisees have developed a collaborative working relationship with their clients. Here I use the concept of 'collaborative empiricism' developed by Beck et al.'s (1979) work in cognitive therapy. The therapeutic style of collaborative empiricism is one in which counsellors endeavour to explain to clients the rationale for most of their interventions. Counsellors and clients set an agenda at most sessions. Counsellors help their clients identify and question maladaptive cognitions through guided discovery. They frequently pause and ask for feedback from clients to determine the impact of their therapeutic interventions, and basically clue clients into most of what is happening in the therapeutic endeavour. I particularly listen for instances where my supervisees do not involve their clients in this way and ask them to reflect on whether this indicates a lack of skill in this area or the presence of dysfunctional attitudes such as low frustration tolerance.

I next concern myself with the question of whether my supervisees' interactive styles present clients with opportunities to reflect on their own dysfunctional interpersonal styles or whether, in fact, the interactive styles of supervisees actually reinforce their clients' interpersonal problems. For example, whilst REBT is an active-directive form of psychotherapy, it is possible for the counsellor to become too active, which is contraindicated particularly with a passive client because it tends to reinforce the client's passivity and hence his or her personal and interpersonal problems.

Finally, I listen for signs of anxiety in my supervisees' interaction with clients and try to help them identify its attitudinal determinants. In my experience, common counsellor problems in this area revolve around the following issues: counsellor need for client approval, counsellor need for competence and to be right, and counsellor need to control the interaction. The effects of such irrational beliefs are invariably harmful for clients and early termination, client deterioration and interminable counselling are the common manifestations of these counsellor problems. In such cases, I usually recommend that the supervisee in question seek psychotherapeutic help to resolve such obstacles to the conduct of effective counselling.

FEEDBACK ON 'GOALS'

Effective counselling is deemed to occur when counsellor and client work towards realizing the client's goals. First, I listen to hear whether my supervisees have elicited their clients' goals for change. Since this often involves considerable negotiation between counsellor and client, I listen for signs that supervisees initiate such negotiation and focus on how they handle the process, which usually occurs at the initial stage of counselling. I also listen to hear whether supervisees help their clients to set goals for a particular session and whether attainment of such goals is feasible. In my experience, effective REBT therapists help their clients see that they can reach their ultimate goals by means of reaching a series of mediating goals. I thus listen for client goals at three levels: (1) session goals, (2) mediating goals and (3) ultimate goals, and most importantly I listen for evidence that counsellors help their clients see the links between them.

The major danger of setting goals at the initial stage of REBT is that trainee counsellors then assume that these goals are relevant to clients for the entire course of counselling. Since their relevance often becomes outdated, I listen for evidence that supervisees periodically review client goals, and whether they strive to understand the psychological processes underlying the shifts that occur.

I listen to what level of goal specificity supervisees are prepared to work with. Clients can state their goals very broadly, e.g. 'I want to be happy', or very specifically, e.g. 'I want to meet three girls by 24 August.' Counsellor errors occur at both levels of specificity. I encourage trainee counsellors to consider the value of medium-range goals, e.g. 'I want to be able to approach girls, still feel concerned about being rejected but without feeling devastated by the prospect.'

Finally, I listen for evidence that supervisees have accepted goals that realistically cannot be achieved by counselling. In my experience as a supervisor these form two clusters. The first cluster of unrealistic goals accepted by trainee counsellors are those that would be more appropriate for computers not humans. Thus, clients whose goals are never to feel anxiety, depression, anger, or who always want to be happy, are doomed to disappointment by even the most talented counsellor. The second cluster of unrealistic client goals accepted by supervisees involves changes in other people of circumstances. This area is more complicated because counsellors had better help clients try non-manipulatively to influence others and circumstances were appropriate, without appearing to promise that such changes are possible. Thus, I encourage my supervisees to help clients deal with unchanging others or circumstances first before discussing attempts to bring about change in them. This point is particularly pertinent to the field of couple counselling.

FEEDBACK ON 'TASKS'

The tasks of REBT therapists can be grouped into a number of major clusters. The first important cluster is concerned with *structuring* therapy. When listening to tapes, I focus and comment on how supervisees structure therapy for their clients. Most specifically, I listen to whether and how supervisees execute the following tasks: (1) the task of outlining their own tasks and that of their clients in counselling; (2) the task of specifying the existing boundaries which frame therapeutic work (e.g. time, geography, frequency of contact and finance); and (3) the task of eliciting and dealing with clients' expectations and misconceptions about counselling. I further concern myself with how supervisees structure each particular counselling session. Questions which are at the forefront of my mind here are the following:

1   Do counsellors set an agenda and/or help clients prioritize items, and how do they do this?
2   Do they use the agenda in a flexible way, dealing with important items that emerge during the course of the session or do they stick rigidly to the agenda, no matter what?
3   Do they deal with their client's experiences concerning any homework assignments arising from the prior session and in particular elicit and deal with reasons for non-completion of such assignments?

4 Do they elicit their client's cooperation throughout the session
   and elicit feedback from clients during and at the end of the
   session?
5 Do they explain their rationale for the interventions that they
   have made in the session or do they intervene without
   explanation?

The second cluster of tasks concerns *assessment*. Effective REBT
depends heavily on adequate assessment of client problems. I pay a
lot of attention to this phase of therapy. Assessment is best carried
out in REBT when trainee counsellors ask clients for specific
examples of their problems. Having elicited specific examples of their
clients' problems, including the most relevant inferences about the
pertinent activating events, supervisees preferably should turn their
attention to the elicitation of clear statements of client's emotional
experiences. Vague formulations of emotional experiences, such as 'I
felt upset' or 'I felt bad' are to be avoided, since they do not provide
enough clarity for identification of mediating irrational beliefs. If
clients' problems are behavioural in nature, clear assessment of
behavioural patterns is indicated. Supervisees preferably should then
proceed to help their clients see that irrational beliefs underlie their
dysfunctional emotional experiences and/or behavioural patterns. I
then listen for evidence that trainee counsellors elicit their clients'
reactions to this formulation of their problems. I give clear feedback
to supervisees concerning their errors at this stage, since mistakes
here are bound to lead to roadblocks later on in the session. Because
a limited number of irrational beliefs are likely to underlie many
client problems, I listen for evidence that trainee counsellors help
their clients see links between their problems, thus enabling clients to
begin to assess their own problems in REBT terms.

Another important component in this cluster concerns assessment
of client progress on all pertinent problems. Ongoing assessment of
progress can be included as an ever-present item on the therapeutic
agenda or periodic review sessions can be conducted. Trainee REBT
therapists often do not carry out this ongoing assessment and thus lose
track of their clients' current status. I often recommend that my
supervisees do this routinely. Ongoing assessment has the additional
advantage of providing opportunities for reformulation of client
goals. One particular feature of assessment which trainee counsellors
often overlook is thorough assessment of suicidal ideation and intent
in depressed patients. If it is dealt with at all, supervisees are often
wary of dealing with this issue directly, preferring to ask such
questions as: 'Have you thought of doing something silly?' Listening
to how trainee counsellors deal with suicide issues often reveals their

own distorted inferences and irrational beliefs concerning these issues. I frequently ask my supervisees to reflect on their own possible dysfunctional attitudes to the introduction of the topic of assessing suicidal ideation and intent. They report such attitudes as: 'I didn't want to upset the client', 'I was too embarrassed to talk about it' and 'I didn't want to put ideas into her head.' When such attitudes are expressed, an ongoing period of dialogue is highly desirable and, if feasible, I encourage the supervisee in question to telephone me so this can occur. If this is not feasible then I recommend that my supervisee contact a clinician who is experienced in treating suicidal clients.

The third cluster of tasks concerns helping clients to re-examine distorted inferences and irrational beliefs. Ideally, trainee counsellors involve clients in this process as much as possible by means of Socratic dialogues. The purpose here is to stimulate clients' own thinking concerning the dysfunctional nature of their cognitive processes. Common trainee errors here usually involve counsellors explaining to their clients why an inference is distorted or why a belief is irrational, and providing them with plausible alternatives instead of allowing those clients who are capable of performing this task to re-examine for themselves the untenable bases for these dysfunctional cognitions. Particularly while trainee counsellors engage their clients in the process of re-examining their irrational beliefs, I listen for evidence that they help their clients see the link between the alternative rational belief and their realistic goals, i.e. how they would like to feel and behave. It is only when clients see this link that they are motivated to work and change their irrational beliefs. Again trainee counsellors often omit this stage.

During the re-examination stage of counselling, trainee REBT therapists can use a variety of cognitive, imagery, emotive and behavioural techniques (Wessler and Wessler, 1980). When I listen to the techniques employed by supervisees, I focus and comment on the following:

I comment on the *variety of techniques* that my supervisees employ over time. Here the greater the variety of techniques which they have in their armamentarium, the more likely it is that they are going to be successful in helping a broad range of clients. If trainee counsellors use a limited range of techniques I try to ascertain the reasons for this. If they indicate that they only know a certain range of techniques, I often suggest others and model their possible applications. However, trainees are often aware of other techniques but do not use them for other reasons. For example, one supervisee claimed that she did not use imagery techniques because she had great difficulty imagining events herself. My task here is to help supervisees identify and correct such blocks.

I comment on my supervisees' *skill* at using particular techniques. Here I both directly comment on the way trainee counsellors employ the techniques and ask them to think of different ways of using them. I may model other ways of using such techniques or suggest to my supervisees that they listen to counselling sessions in the Institute for Rational-Emotive Therapy's tape library in which such techniques are skilfully demonstrated.

I comment on the *relevant* use of particular techniques. Sometimes trainee counsellors employ techniques skilfully but inappropriately. Here supervisees often do not give enough thought to the use of techniques with specific clients with whom they are working. This danger is partially avoided if they explain adequately their rationale for using particular techniques and gain client cooperation beforehand. If clients cannot see a technique's relevance, this is one sign that perhaps it should not be used. In addition, trainee counsellors' choice of technique may be inappropriate for the modality of experience concerned. For example, if a particular client's irrational belief is manifested in imagery, then re-examination through verbal dialogue may not be as relevant as a carefully selected imagery method. Knowledge of client's dominant modalities is important here.

The final cluster of tasks concerns the use of *homework assignments*. Homework exercises are important in REBT because their appropriate use helps clients to generalize their learning from the counselling situation to everyday experience. I listen carefully to the following:

I focus on the amount of time that trainee counsellors devote to discussing possible assignments with their clients. A common fault here is that trainees devote too little time to this and consequently terminate the session either by unilaterally assigning homework exercises – a procedure which often increases the possibility of client resistance – or by dropping the subject altogether. Here I usually ask my supervisees to consider how much time to devote to the process of assigning homework and to monitor closely their performance on this parameter.

I focus on how adequately trainee counsellors prepare their clients for doing assignments. Important considerations here concern:

(a) the relevance of the tasks to the issues that have hopefully been thoroughly assessed and re-examined in the session in question;
(b) clients seeing clearly the potential value of such assignments to their mediating and ultimate goals;
(c) clients being fully involved by trainee counsellors in the negotiation of homework assignments.

I listen carefully for evidence that supervisees have tried to uncover possible obstacles to the successful completion of assignments by asking their clients in advance to speculate on what might stop them from carrying them out. If relevant information is uncovered by such enquiry, I listen to how trainees help their clients overcome such obstacles in the session. If this information is not asked for, I suggest to them that they think of the value of doing this routinely.

I listen for evidence that trainee counsellors engage clients in rehearsal of homework assignments either in imagery or using behavioural rehearsal in the session. This enables clients to gain some related experience of doing assignments and may in itself unearth further dysfunctional cognitions which might prevent clients from completing such tasks in their everyday situation.

I listen to the specificity of negotiated homework assignments. The more tasks have been specified, the more likely it is that clients will be able to carry them out successfully.

I listen to the breadth of assignments suggested by trainee counsellors to their clients over the supervisory period. Preferably, if appropriate, a wide range of behavioural, emotive, written and imagery assignments should be used during counselling. If trainees are employing a narrow range of tasks, I try and discern the reasons for this and encourage them to think about remedying this.

In addition, throughout the supervisory period, I encourage my supervisees to encourage their clients to move towards independence so that they in fact acquire the skills to be their own counsellors. If this is not done, I try and discover the reasons and encourage trainees to reflect on possible motivations that they might have for encouraging dependence. I attempt to sensitize my supervisees to the problem of client resistance to change and to possible reasons for this. Resistance may stem from client problems, counsellor problems, poor counsellor skills or their interaction.

Finally, I endeavour to communicate my points to supervisees in the form of hypotheses for them to consider and possibly test. I encourage them to give me feedback on any suggestions that I have made and on my style of supervision in general so that I can fit the supervisory experience to individual supervisee requirements.

References

Beck, A.T., Rush, A.J., Shaw, B.F. and Emery, G. (1979) *Cognitive Therapy of Depression*. New York: Guilford Press.

Dryden, W. (1982) 'The therapeutic alliance: conceptual issues and some research findings', *Midland Journal of Psychotherapy*, 1: 14–19.

Garcia, E. (1976) 'Supervision of therapists'. Unpublished lecture given at the Institute for Advanced Study of Rational-Emotive Therapy, New York City, 11 July.

Rogers, C.R. (1957) 'The necessary and sufficient conditions of therapeutic personality change', *Journal of Consulting Psychology*, 21: 95–103.

Wessler, R.L. and Ellis, A. (1980) 'Supervision in rational-emotive therapy', in A.K. Hess (ed.), *Psychotherapy Supervision*. New York: Wiley.

Wessler, R.A. and Wessler, R.L. (1980) *The Principles and Practice of Rational-Emotive Therapy*. San Francisco: Jossey-Bass.

12

Supervision of REBT Therapists: The Thirteen-Step Self-Supervision Inventory

by Robin Yapp and Windy Dryden

The practice of rational emotive behaviour therapy (REBT) in the United Kingdom and Ireland, although gaining in popularity over recent years, continues to be adopted by a minority of health professionals. It is not surprising therefore, that the number of REBT supervisors of a suitable calibre is also limited. For both experienced practitioners and novice trainees, this represents a significant problem. The current professional code of practice for REBT therapists in the UK established by the Association for Rational Emotive Behaviour Therapists (AREBT, 1991), in keeping with the BAC Code of conduct (BAC, 1990) recommends that each therapist fulfil a mandatory requirement of 1.5 hours supervision per calendar month. With the dearth of qualified REBT professionals in the UK, who then provides the supervision? This chapter seeks to highlight the current options available to REBT therapists, and then outline a basic framework for self-supervision which may prove a useful adjunct to practitioners' existing arrangements.

There are many different models of supervision available to the therapist, which are common to many differing theoretical approaches; Feltham and Dryden, (1994) provide an excellent in-depth discussion on this subject. However, if we practise as REBT therapists, then we require supervision of that approach from another experienced REBT practitioner. Anything less may not address the technical ability of the supervisee in an adequate fashion. Albert Ellis's views on supervision appear to support this, as Dryden (1991: 92) notes: Ellis suggests 'a periodic supervisory relationship between recently trained and more experienced REBT therapists'. At present, the supervisory options for REBT therapists are currently one or a combination of the following:

- Obtain the supervisory requirement by face-to-face supervision with a recognized REBT supervisor.

This chapter was written by Robin Yapp and Windy Dryden and first published in *The Rational Emotive Behaviour Therapist*, 1994, 2(1): 16–24.

- Obtain supervision through postal audio-tape supervision with a recognized REBT supervisor.
- Obtain telephone-based supervision from a recognized REBT supervisor.
- Obtain face-to-face supervision (or postal audio-tape supervision) through co-supervision (peer group).
- Obtain group supervision by peers (face to face).
- Obtain telephone supervision by peer group.
- Enrol in an REBT training programme where supervision is provided.

These methods are not confined to the UK; for example, postal audio-tape supervision could be arranged with a REBT professional overseas (see Chapter 11).

It is of course desirable for REBT therapists to obtain supervision in excess of the minimum requirement established by AREBT, and whilst the above options may represent a significant financial investment by the therapist, there is another option which can be added to the above list, and that method is self-supervision.

The supervision of one's own work, is, of course, not sufficient in itself to maintain the ethical and professional standards that a qualified REBT supervisor could provide, and the authors would not wish the reader to think otherwise. However, it can and does provide a useful and insightful addition to formal supervisory arrangements. Wessler and Wessler (1980) and Walen, DiGiuseppe and Dryden, (1992) provide supervisory guidelines for the REBT therapist to consider, and although what follows, based on these works, is not a comprehensive listing, it may prove to be a useful trigger for self-analysis of your own therapeutic work with clients. The emphasis in this instance is on questioning and providing justification for the work you carry out at each stage of the REBT counselling sequence. REBT operates from a scientist-practitioner approach, so we should be able to justify each intervention we make.

What are the First Steps in Self-Supervision?

In REBT, as with many other schools of therapy such as cognitive-behaviour therapy (CBT), therapists tape-record their counselling work. Although this has become a familiar aspect of REBT counselling, and is considered standard practice (Corsini and Wedding, 1989) the authors are surprised at the reluctance exhibited by some REBT therapists concerning the tape-recording of their work. There are many benefits of recording of counselling sessions, for example:

- Either replaying the tape either outside the counselling sessions or replaying particular sections within subsequent sessions can assist the client's learning. As Dryden and Yankura (1993) note, clients can often become confused during therapy sessions, and the replaying of session tapes helps clarify and reinforce rational concepts.
- It can help maintain professional standards (therapists may be less likely to act unethically if the sessions are recorded).
- It can provide a medium to take to formal individual or group supervision that has greater accuracy than written notes, etc.

The recording of client work also represents an ideal basis on which to build a self-supervision programme. The recorded session can be replayed and evaluated by the therapist thus providing evidence of *what* was carried out during the session, rather than the therapist's own inferences about what occurred, which may or may not be true. Further discussion on the merits of tape-recorded sessions and trainee/supervisee anxieties about this can be found in Dryden (1987).

Having established what the therapist can assess, we can now consider the types of question we can ask in order to effect a self-supervision process. This self-supervision framework has been based upon the REBT counselling sequence (Dryden, 1990). In supervising your own work with clients, first consider the issues relating to the 'Overview of the Counselling Session' (Part 1 of the Thirteen-Step Self-Supervision Inventory); secondly, with these issues in mind, establish at which point in the sequence you believe that you were working with the client in the session and refer to the appropriate section in Part 2 of the inventory.

The thirteen-step self-supervision inventory is a stimulus for reflection on the counselling session, rather than a comprehensive list of all the issues to cover. It is not intended as a replacement for formal supervision. It is hoped that this inventory will assist both novice and experienced therapists in providing efficient and effective REBT to their clients.

The Thirteen-Step Self-Supervision Inventory: Part 1

Consider the following questions and provide evidence from the counselling session to substantiate your answers. If you experience difficulty in addressing any of the questions, it is recommended that you raise these with your REBT supervisor.

OVERVIEW OF COUNSELLING SESSION

How much focus did you place on developing the therapeutic relationship? Was this appropriate or at the expense of task activities?

How did you adapt your therapeutic style to the needs of your client? Was this effective? What else could you have done to improve on this?

Did you help your client understand what tasks you and your client need to accomplish in counselling and how these relate to your client's goals?

Did you identify and address your client's doubts about his or her ability to work towards his or her goals?

Is there any evidence that you judged or rated your client as a whole, or that the client rated you as a whole?

Did you answer your client's questions fully and in a non-defensive, open manner?

Did you use vocabulary that was suitable for your client? Give reasons why you considered it was/was not appropriate.

To what extent was your approach didactic rather than Socratic? What was your rationale for this?

Did you ask your client to articulate his or her understanding of the learning points made at suitable stages within the session?

Did you identify and address your client's priorities?

Did you set an agenda and keep to it? If not, what are your reasons for not doing so, and how could you address these in future?

Did you involve the client in all stages of the counselling process?

Did you run over the allotted time? What were your reasons for this?

How many key points did you teach in the session? How many key points did your client understand at the end of the session?

The Thirteen-Step Self-Supervision Inventory: Part 2

1 ASK FOR A PROBLEM

Did you use relevant questions to elicit information regarding your client's specific problems, life situation, expectations of therapy, without obtaining too much information?

Did you focus on one target problem, or did you switch from one to another in quick succession? How could you have improved the focus?

2 DEFINE AND AGREE THE TARGET PROBLEM (SET GOALS IN LINE WITH THE PROBLEM AS DEFINED)

What were the client's goals for therapy?

Were the goals specific and appropriate?

How did you ensure the client was made aware of the distinction between a healthy and an unhealthy feeling?

How did you help your client distinguish between short- and long-term goals?

3 ASSESS C

How did you establish that your client's C was an inappropriate response?

What evidence did you obtain to support this fact?

Could this have been done more effectively? If so, what other methods could you have used instead?

What was your hypothesis regarding the client's specific and core irrational beliefs at this stage?

4 ASSESS A

How did you assess A?

Could this have been done more effectively? What other methods could you have used instead?

5 DETERMINE WHETHER OR NOT YOUR CLIENT HAS A SECONDARY EMOTIONAL PROBLEM (AND ASSESS IF APPROPRIATE)

What evidence (if any) did you find to indicate a secondary problem?

Did you explain to your client your rationale for working on the secondary problem first?

Did you obtain explicit agreement from the client to switch focus to the secondary problem?

Outline your client's disturbance chain, and describe how this influenced your treatment strategy.

6 TEACH THE B–C CONNECTION

What method did you use to teach the B–C connection?

Was this relevant to the client's circumstances?

If not, how could you have tailored your example more effectively?

To what extent was the method you employed effective?

What errors did you make in teaching the B–C connection?

What will you need to do in future to prevent these errors recurring?

7   ASSESS IB

Did you assess the client's full irrational belief (premise and derivative/s)?

How did you ensure that you did not 'put words into the client's mouth'?

How did you ensure that the selected IB was the most clinically relevant IB?

8   CONNECT IB AND C

Did you Socratically question your client concerning the IB–C connection within the context of his or her goals?

Did you Socratically question your client concerning the RB–C connection within the context of his or her goals?

9   DISPUTE IB

Did you combine empirical, logical and pragmatic disputes?

Did you separately dispute the premise, before attempting to dispute the derivative? In which style (humorous, enactive, metaphorical, didactic, Socratic) did you dispute? Explain why you chose to adopt one or a combination of these styles for your client. How successful was this?

How did you ensure that the process of disputing was kept meaningful for your client?

Did you assist your client to consider the evidence against his or her IBs but *in support* of his or her rational beliefs?

Did you allow your client adequate thinking time to respond to your questions?

Did you alternate your disputing between the specific and abstract IBs held by your client? If so, why did you do this?

Did you help your client to understand the difference between a conditional must and an absolute must?

Did you use self-disclosure? If so, how relevant was this, and how did your client react?

How forcefully did your client dispute his or her irrational beliefs? How can you encourage your client to dispute more forcefully?

10 PREPARE YOUR CLIENT TO DEEPEN HIS OR HER
CONVICTION IN HIS OR HER RATIONAL BELIEFS

How did you communicate to your client that it would be necessary for him or her to work inside and outside of the therapy sessions?

Did you ensure that your client understands the issues involved in moving from intellectual insight to emotional insight? What evidence do you have to support your answer?

Did you seek to assess any subtle client behaviours that might counter the benefits of therapy?

11 HOMEWORK ASSIGNMENTS

What was the primary target of the homework task (e.g. ego disturbance or discomfort disturbance)?

Was the homework assignment related to what was discussed in the session?

Did you provide your client with a rationale for completing the homework assignment?

Was the homework task related specifically to your client's problem?

Did you negotiate the homework task with your client?

Did you rehearse the execution of the homework task with your client?

Did you identify obstacles to completion of the homework task, and help your client prepare to overcome these?

What evidence do you have to demonstrate that the homework task you negotiated would be *challenging, but not overwhelming* for your client?

Which, if any, self-help forms did you use with your client? What were your reasons for using the form/s? Did you educate your client in its use?

12 CHECK HOMEWORK ASSIGNMENTS

If your client failed to carry out the homework assignment, did you (a) ensure that the reasons were identified, and (b) identify ways in which these could be addressed?

What evidence do you have that your client faced A and disputed his or her IB?

Did you reinforce your client's understanding of the learning outcomes of completing the task within the context of his or her goals?

Did your client make any errors in completing the task, and did you correct them?

Did your client complete the task to gain your approval? If so, how might you address this?

13   FACILITATE THE WORKING-THROUGH PROCESS

What evidence do you have to demonstrate that your client has integrated his or her rational beliefs into his or her emotional and behavioural repertoire? How could you help your client improve on this?

How did you help your client to apply a rational philosophy to other areas of his or her life?

How did you enable your client to assess his or her level of change?

Did you teach your client relapse prevention? How was this done? How could you improve on this?

References

AREBT (1991) *Code of Practice*. Birmingham: Association for Rational-Emotive Behaviour Therapists.

BAC (1990) *Code of Ethics and Practice for Counsellors*. Rugby: British Association for Counselling.

Corsini, R.J. and Wedding, D. (1989) *Current Psychotherapies*, 4th edn. Itasca, IL: F.E. Peacock.

Dryden, W. (1987) *Current Issues in Rational-Emotive Therapy*. London: Croom Helm.

Dryden, W. (1990) *Rational-Emotive Counselling in Action*. London: Sage.

Dryden, W. (1991) *A Dialogue with Albert Ellis: Against Dogma*. Buckingham: Open University Press.

Dryden, W. and Yankura, J. (1993) *Counselling Individuals: A Rational-Emotive Handbook*, 2nd edn. London: Whurr.

Feltham, C. and Dryden, W. (1994) *Developing Counsellor Supervision*. London: Sage.

Walen, S., DiGiuseppe, R. and Dryden, W. (1992) *A Practitioner's Guide to Rational-Emotive Therapy*, 2nd edn. New York: Oxford University Press.

Wessler, R.A. and Wessler R.L. (1980) *The Principles and Practice of Rational-Emotive Therapy*. San Francisco: Jossey-Bass.

Index

As: *see* activating event

ABC model, 34; application, 87; and concurrent belief model , 86–98; expanded (ABCDE) form, 22–3, 86–7; need for clients to understand, 101; relationship between elements, 23, 70–84; and secondary disturbance, 87–9

action tendencies, 14–20, 21–2, 66, 82–3

activating events (As), 22, 34; actual and inferred, 74–5; assessment of, 161; and Bs, 75–7, 77–8; emotions and, 81–3; Gs and, 70–1; inferred As and behavioural Cs, 78–9

all-or-nothing thinking, 130

anger, 110; action tendencies, 15, 66, 82–3; and evaluative thinking, 34; healthy, 15; response options, 67–8; unhealthy, 15

anorgasmia, 58

anti-awfulizing, 5–6

anxiety, 14, 110; behavioural strategies to avoid, 54–5, 57–8; and belief structures, 91–2; ego and discomfort disturbance in, 11; impact of behaviour on, 84; as self-fulfilling prophecy, 41; supervision, 126–43; in trainees' interaction with clients, 150

approval, need for boss's, 47–8

assessment: of As, 161; of Cs, 93–6, 161; of iBs, 162; of level of functioning, 102; supervisees' use of, 152–3

audio-tape recordings: benefits of, 158–9; disputing on, 121–2; in supervision, 126–43, 145–55

auto-erotic asphyxia, 59

awfulizing, 5–6, 36–7, 76; *see also* secondary irrational beliefs

Bs: *see* beliefs

'backsliding', 96–7

Beck, Aaron, 13, 130, 149

behaviour/behavioural Cs, 51–69; Gs and, 73–4; impact on beliefs, 80–1; impact on emotions, 84; inferred As and, 78–9; relationship with cognition and emotion, 23, 32–3

behavioural change, 42

behavioural competence, 68–9

behavioural methods, 122–4

beliefs (Bs, iBs, rBs), 22, 34; actual As and, 75–7; assessment of irrational, 162; B–C connection, 161–2; belief pairs, 4–8; concurrent belief model, 86–98; deepening of rational, 163; Gs and, 71–2; iB–C connection, 162; impact of behaviour on, 80–1; impact of emotions on, 80; impact on emotions, 145; inferred As and, 77–8; irrational, in trainees, 134–5; rational and irrational, 3, 13–21; supervisees' work with irrational, 153; use of secondary irrational in determining type of disturbance, 47–50

binging, 60

biology, and disturbance, 40

Bordin, E.S., 25

brief REBT: client suitability, 99–103; contraindications, 103–4

Budman, S.H., 104

Burns, D.D., 130

Cs: *see* consequences

Casey, A., 135

catastrophes, 36–7, 75–6

cognition: relationship with emotion and behaviour, 23, 32–3; types of, 3–4, 33–4

cognitive consequences of negative emotions, 14–20, 21

cognitive revolution, 2

cold cognitions, 33